Caitlin has [illegible] people dealing with feelings of defeat. Her ability to use stories and illustrations is a true gift that I believe helps people see spiritual truths. In Leaving Defeat, she helps equip you with ways to begin walking in victory. I pray God uses her book to help you begin living the life you were meant to live.

Robert Andrews

Pastor, Elevate Church of Vicksburg, Mississippi

Leaving Defeat

Illuminating the path to victory

Caitlin Childs

Book Cover by Alvin Foster.

IBSN: (Paperback) 979-8-9896048-5-2

IBSN: (E-book) 979-8-9896048-6-9

Contents

To my husband, Joshua,

Who saw me when I was invisible and loved me when I was defeated.

It is an honor to be your wife.

Consider it pure joy, my brothers and sisters, whenever you face trials of many kinds, because you know that the testing of your faith produces perseverance. Let perseverance finish its work so that you may be mature and complete, not lacking anything.

James 1:2-4

Introduction

I sat in our church's Wednesday night Bible study one night, listening to the preacher teach on the book of Revelation. One thing he said in particular really stuck out to me. "If the devil and his demons knew that crucifying Jesus would have led to their ultimate demise, do you think they would have fought so hard to make it happen? No, but God hid His victory inside that supposed defeat."[1]

I started thinking about my own life. How many times I had felt defeated. Too heartbroken to keep living. Too afraid to move forward. I thought about the times when it was almost too difficult to get out of bed because of depression. The times when betrayal left me feeling like I had no value. And then I thought about how each and every time, God brought me through that hardship and into a place of victory. The thing is, he does seem to have a pattern of hiding his victories behind a veil of defeat. Whenever we are in a place where we feel like we can't possibly

---

1. Pastor Robert Andrews, Elevate Church, Vicksburg, Mississippi.

overcome our circumstances, that's usually when God swoops in and unveils the victory that's been there all along.

Listen, one thing I want you to understand about what you're getting ready to read is that this book is not a quick fix for all of your problems. It's not a way to fast-track you to success. It's definitely not a cure for serious mental struggles or a substitute for professional help. This book is simply a compilation of my stories. These are my testimonies about how God brought me from a place of darkness and into the light. I figured if God is asking me to share these stories, He must have something that he wants you to learn from them too.

I will warn you though, that this journey isn't an easy one. If you want to defeat the giants in your life, you're going to have to face them first. Throughout this book, you're going to come face to face with some very raw, very real, very personal stories. And chances are that one or two of them will remind you of a story in your own life that you wish you could forget. At some point, you're probably going to even be tempted to put the book down and never pick it up again. If and when you get to that point, I want you to remember something. There is nothing you can't do with Jesus by your side.

Yes, this may spark some painful memories, but the way I see it, it's like healing a broken bone. When a bone breaks, the first thing the doctors have to do is set it so that the bone can heal properly. If a bone heals incorrectly, it can cause a multitude of other problems down the road. And sometimes, if the bone has already "healed" but wasn't set properly, the doctor will have to re-break it and reset it in order to fix the complications that the wound was causing.

There always seems to be a breaking before a breakthrough. New wine comes from the crushing of the grapes. Fresh oil comes from the pressing of the olives. If we want the new wine, the fresh oil, and the healed wounds, sometimes that means having to go through the crushing, the pressing, and the breaking to get there. But just because it's difficult doesn't mean it's not worth it.

Remember the parable Jesus told about the man who found treasure in the field? The story is found in Matthew 13:44. "The kingdom of heaven is like treasure hidden in a field. When a man found it, he hid it again, and then in his joy went and sold all he had and bought that field." You see, this man understood something we can all learn from. When you're following God, everything you give up is far less valuable than everything you'll get back. No, it's not easy to let go of everything you've ever known. It's not easy to change all of the old mindsets that have been holding you back for decades. But it is well worth it.

There are, however, dangers of staying where we are. If we continue to live a life where we choose our comfort over our calling, we miss out on all of that treasure and fruitfulness that God wants to bring forth. In Matthew 19, we see Jesus telling a rich young ruler to sell everything he has to come and follow him. The rich young ruler can't do it. He's too set in his ways, too comfortable. He chose to stick to *what* he knows rather than sticking to *who* he knows.

The beautiful thing about God is that He always gives us a choice. He won't pin you into a corner and force you to choose the option that He knows is best for you. Why do you think He put the tree of knowledge of good and evil in the Garden of Eden if He didn't want Adam and Eve to eat from it? It's because He always wants to give us an option to obey him. And now, you're faced with a similar choice. Will you cling to what you know? Will you continue to tighten your grip on the mindsets and habits that have been holding you back for most of your life? Or will you make the hard choice–the scary choice–and work your way towards victory? Will you be the rich young ruler, or the man that finds treasure in the field?

Make no mistake. If you choose to follow Jesus down this path, it's going to cost you everything. But what you will get back is *everything and then some.* So if you're tired of being pushed around by the situations in your life, by the loneliness that cripples you, or the fears in your mind that replay on a loop, and if you're tired of feeling like hell is doing its best to kill you, just remember, there's always victory behind the defeat. All you have to do is set out to find it.

Chapter One

Transformation

When I was in elementary school, I used to love checking under the picnic tables on the playground. Every now and then, I would get lucky enough to find the treasure I was searching for: a little cocoon nestled safely in the shade of the splintering pine wood. A couple of times, I was even allowed to take these cocoons home with me. I would find a mason jar and get my dad to poke holes in the top to form a makeshift cage. Then I would set it on my bedside table and watch for any signs of movement as I drifted off to sleep. One night, I was awakened by a scratching noise. I rubbed the sleep out of my eyes and looked over just in time to see a freshly hatched butterfly escaping through one of the holes in the top of the jar. I watched in fascination as the creature that had just been an entirely different insect a few days before began to spread its wings to dry in the dimness of my nightlight. I learned a couple of very valuable things that day. Adversity is never our enemy, and transformation is possible, even in the dark.

Do you want to know what I've noticed? When a caterpillar transforms into a butterfly, it's not an easy process. And it's not cute or fun either. It's messy and hard. Once the caterpillar shuts itself into its little cocoon, it begins the process of quite literally turning to goo. Its whole body has to break down in order to reveal the wings that were hiding inside it the whole time. Then it has to be rearranged into a new creation that can do things the caterpillar never even dreamed were possible. No, there's nothing easy about it. But if it didn't go through that process, it wouldn't be able to fly.

I may not know everything, but I do understand transformation. I've lived it. I've seen how much of a difference it can make when you latch onto the love of God and that love changes you from the inside out. And I am desperately aching to introduce you to it, too. Maybe you've lived a life where no one has made you aware of your potential to fly. Or maybe you've had people encourage you to fly before you had a chance to grow. Either way, I'd like to try and help you undo that damage by taking you through the process I went through. And I won't lie to you, it won't be easy. It won't be quick either. There will be parts of you that break down altogether to make room for something new. But speaking as someone who has been through this process, I can say without a doubt that it is more than worth it. We're not meant to figure everything out on our own. And so, if you've never had anyone hold your hand and show you what's possible, I would be honored to be that person for you.

Transformation is Necessary

In order to start this journey, we need to understand why it's even necessary in the first place. Do you know why caterpillars turn into butterflies? It's because the caterpillar is the larva (or baby stage) of a butterfly. They can't reproduce unless they transform. If they were to stay perpetual caterpillars, their entire insect species would die off. The caterpillars sole purpose is to eat and grow. That's it. Nothing more is expected of the caterpillar until it's ready for the transformation to take place. Nature has a funny way of mirroring the spiritual realm–almost as if it were designed that way. Crazy, right?

During The Great Commission (found in Matthew 28:19-20), Jesus tells His followers to "go and make disciples." In other words, reproduce. The life that has been given to us is meant to be duplicated and shared, not just physically, but spiritually as well. But unless we've gone through that heart transformation ourselves, we are not able to reproduce more disciples. The best we can do is make converts.

I remember a time in my life when I truly could not tell the difference. Butterflies, caterpillars...they all looked the same to me. Spiritually speaking, of course. I was raised in church. My family was there every time the doors were open. And on that fateful night when I was eight years old, our family friend's art ministry came to perform at our church. I was moved so deeply by the story of Jesus told through artwork that I decided I had to do something special to mark the occasion. So I asked Jesus into my heart. After that, I would often hear the preachers say that if you are a Christian, your life is supposed to be transformed. You're a new creation now, so you should be able to tell the difference between your life before Jesus and your life after Jesus. Did I mention that I was *eight?* How was my life supposed to change so drastically? I still did the same things as always. I went to church three times a week with my family and attended every Vacation Bible School and camp they offered. What else was I supposed to do? I just checked that off as one of those "Christian sayings" that must not apply to me or my life.

For the next 21 years, I went around living my life as a convert, not as a disciple. I prayed whenever I thought about it, read my Bible occasionally, and still attended church faithfully. It wasn't until 2020, when my Dad was diagnosed with stomach cancer that I cried out to God and His presence shook the very foundation I was standing on. It was very much a before and after moment; a definitive transformation. And I suddenly realized that accepting Jesus into your life is so much more than saying a prayer. It's starting a relationship. The kind of relationship that rocks your world and never leaves you the same way it found you. And yet, we walk around in a world full of Christians that have never experienced that transformation. A lot of churches are crawling with caterpillars and they don't even know it.

So how do we fix this? First, it's important to identify where you are in this process. Are you a caterpillar? If so, your sole mission is to learn and grow. If you've already gone through the transformation and become a butterfly, then I sure hope you realize that you are on assignment. It's cute to watch sweet little butterflies flitting around from flower to flower. But what we don't often realize is that they are hunters. They are in a time crunch. You see, they only have less than a month to accomplish their mission in life. So they hunt for nectar and hunt for a mate, taking time to rest when necessary. Just because your transformation is complete doesn't mean your assignment is. In fact, you're just getting started.

Transformation is Achievable

As a parent, one of the hardest lessons I've had to learn is that my kids have to learn to do things for themselves. It's so much easier (and honestly, faster) to help them put on their shoes or open their snacks. But once my second child was born, I realized that I couldn't do it all, and that I was going to have to start delegating some of the responsibility. The only problem was that my son is and always has been a little bit of a perfectionist. When he was two years old, he started stacking his cars into neat little lines. He still does that to this day. He's the type that wants to be able to do it right the first time, or not do it at all.

Having him begin to do things on his own was a test of patience for both of us. Many tears were shed from both parties. Until one day, I discovered something that seemed to work. He was trying to put his shoes on by himself. He was getting frustrated, and a meltdown was brewing on the horizon. I stopped him, knelt down to his level, and made eye contact. After a few deep breaths,

I said, "Buddy, you can do this. Every time you don't get it right, I want you to say the words, 'I can do this if I just keep trying.'"

He took a deep breath and decided to make another attempt. His heel slipped to the side and he lost his grip. Another deep breath. Through clenched teeth and restricted tears, he said, "I can do this if I just keep trying." He tried again. This time, the resistance caused the shoe to fling off of his foot entirely. His head hung. Deep breath. "I can do this if I just keep trying!" He grabbed the shoe, plopped back down, and took one final deep breath. Success! You would've thought he had just medaled in the Olympics by the way we celebrated that small victory.

I think a lot of people approach transformation the way my son was approaching putting on his shoes by himself. They look at the end result, compare it to their current ability, and decide that failure is inevitable, so why even try? The thing is, failure is not the enemy. Failure is what gets us closer to the end goal.

I love the way that Thomas Edison viewed the subject of failure. Edison is known for his invention of the lightbulb. However, he didn't achieve success with that invention overnight. He had many, many failed attempts before he successfully reached his goal. But Edison didn't see those attempts as failures. Instead, he learned something from each and every attempt that he applied to the next try. He allegedly once described this as a process that had 1,000 steps toward success.[1]

---

1. Paraphrased from alleged interviews with reporters

The way I see it, you have two options when it comes to approaching this journey you're about to embark on. You can let the fear of failure stop you, forever remaining a caterpillar with no intent to ever reproduce. OR, you can view failure as one step closer to the goal. Marathons aren't run all at once, lightbulbs aren't invented overnight, and your transformation isn't any different. But I promise you, you can do this if you just keep trying.

Here's the deal. Stepping into this transformation is going to require faith. I've met a lot of people along my journey, and it's become easier and easier to spot the people who are truly transformed in contrast to the ones who are just going through the motions. Do you know how you can tell? Each and every person who is truly transformed had to take a leap of faith to get there.

Here's another interesting fact about butterflies: they do not have the ability to see their own wings. So how do they know that they possess the ability to fly? My best guess is that there is an instinct within them that tells them they were made for more than crawling on the ground, thinking no further than their next meal. We all have that same instinct. If we want to break out of the mundane cycles of just living our lives going through the motions, it's going to require us to take a leap of faith and trust in the wings we cannot see. It's not enough for us to believe that there's more available to us. We have to *act* on it.

Transformation is Optional

One of the greatest things about God is also one of the saddest things about humans if you ask me. He is so good, and so loving, and so understanding, that He will never, ever force you to change. The sad thing is, He will never force you to change, so most people don't. We all know someone who has used up most of their time on this earth, and is still living with the same issues they had 25, 30, 50 years ago. Why is that? Is it because they didn't want anything to change? Is it because they wanted to struggle with the same cyclical things over and over and over and over? My guess is no.

Here's my theory: I believe that the reason nothing changes for them is because they are expecting the change to happen *TO* them, rather than going out and taking hold of it for themselves. They go through the motions of their daily lives, hoping and praying that one day they will be zapped with the very thing that they seem to be missing, like sitting in front of a nearly finished puzzle, willing the missing pieces to magically appear.

Have you ever seen anyone get into shape and live a healthy lifestyle simply by willing it to happen to them? No, those people get up, deny themselves of the things they want in favor of the things that are best, and put in the work. They get into the gym multiple days a week, fuel their bodies with healthy foods and restrict the things that keep them from their goals. In order to acquire the things you want, you have to do what it takes to get them. I wish I could tell you that it happens automatically. It would be nice if things were that simple and we were quite literally floating through this life, wouldn't it? The truth is that that's not the reality we live in. If that caterpillar doesn't eat and grow, it will never transform. The same goes for you.

I've noticed three main reasons that seem to hold people back from ever changing their ways: fear, comfort, and lack of motivation. Or maybe even a combination of the three. People either fear the unknown, they're comfortable where they are and don't see a reason to change, or they know that they would benefit from some level of growth, but they lack the discipline to move toward that growth for one reason or another. If I haven't made it obvious yet, that bothers me. Do you want to know why it bothers me? Because I lived it. And while I was living it, nobody seemed to have a problem with it. I didn't have anyone take me under their wing, look me in the eyes, and tell me that my complacency was going to kill me faster than anything else could. I was allowed to drown in my ignorance. It wasn't for lack of education that I was drowning, just a lack of discipleship. It was a lack of people walking me through what they were teaching me. Why do you think I'm so passionate about getting these books into as many hands as possible? It's because if no one else will, I will disciple you. You are my baby chick now, tucked under my wing and I would rather die than watch you drown.

I recently heard Priscilla Shirer tell a story about when this really clicked in her brain. She said she was at the mall with her youngest son and they were riding the escalator up to the second floor. Except, when she looked down by her side, her son wasn't there. Instead, she found him on the opposite escalator headed down towards the first floor, walking up the steps as they came to him. Through gritted teeth, she told her son to ride that escalator down to the first floor and get back on the correct escalator. As he stopped moving, she watched him effortlessly descend.[2] And then it hit her. This world is quite literally going to hell in a handbasket. You can thank sin for that. As soon as sin entered the world due to a misuse of free will, this ship started sinking. We don't get a choice between heaven and hell. We are all bound for hell. We get a choice on whether we want to jump off the sinking ship and accept the life raft that has been offered to us or not. The same is true for our mindsets. Our brains will naturally drift towards some really detrimental patterns, and if we don't take charge of the situation and make the necessary course corrections to get it under control, we'll find ourselves stuck in the same ruts and have even more difficulty breaking free.

When you have this perspective shift, you now become desperate to make other people aware of it as well, preferably without causing them too much alarm. So when people say that they are afraid of change, I tend to think "*and you're not afraid to stay here?*" When people say that they are comfortable the way they are and don't feel the need to change, I think "*and nobody's made you aware of the dangers of that?*" And when people say they know they need to change but are just struggling to be motivated

---

2. The Candace Cameron Bure Podcast, Season 8 with Priscilla Shirer

enough to make those lifestyle shifts, it's difficult not to picture them on the Titanic, sleeping or scrolling their phones as the water rises up to their neck.

Listen, I don't mean to alarm you because I know this sounds intense. The truth is, it is intense. I won't lie to you and tell you that a life with God is all sunshine and rainbows. What I will tell you is that you go from sitting on the bench to being point guard on the winning team. Yes, it's going to take effort. Yes, there will be sweat, blood, and tears involved. But the last thing I want is for you to exit this life and *then* realize how much more was available to you. I love you enough to want you to experience it all now, while you still have the chance to make a difference for others and for yourself.

I'm going to ask you to do me a favor. I want you to take the time to ask yourself some really hard questions. See? I told you you would want to shut this book and never return. That was fast, wasn't it? If you're still reading and willing to be challenged, take a moment to ask yourself what things you are struggling with now that you have continually struggled with for the last year, or five years, or ten years. What are the recurring issues that keep popping up? Maybe you feel like every time you open up to people, you're met with rejection. Or maybe you feel like no matter how hard you try to make people happy, it's still never enough. If something comes to mind, don't worry. It just means you've pinpointed the area where you can grow the most. I'm not going to leave you alone in this. We're going to walk through it together and cover so many of these issues in the chapters ahead. You've probably been trapped in that cycle for far too long. It's time to get you out.

Chapter Two

Unpack Your Bag

I love watching videos of people restoring old, broken down furniture. It's so much fun to see life restored back into something that was once discarded. When they take an old, chipped wood dresser with the doors barely hanging on its hinges and transform it so well that you can't even tell it was ever broken; it just gives me such a rush of dopamine. As I've watched these videos, I've noticed that they all start with the same first step. They remove the old finish. Your transformation process is going to be much the same way. I know a lot of people want to be handed a sword right up front and join the fight immediately. And while I appreciate your enthusiasm, we need to do this in the right order. First, we're going to be building our foundation, then we can start to shed off those old mindsets that have been holding you back. That's where we "scrape off the old finish" before equipping you with a new one. Like I said before, I know this process isn't fun, but if you can stick with it until the end, you will be more than prepared for the fight.

Before we can set out on our quest to victory, we have to first acknowledge how we're going to get there. This requires us to take a deep, hard look into what we actually believe. Now, this part may be difficult. Because as you set out on this adventure, you're inevitably going to be met with situation after situation that requires you to analyze what you believe under a microscope and see if it's actually true or not. Do you really believe that your fears are keeping you safe? Or is it possible that they're holding you back? Do you really believe that God is only pleased with you when you're not rocking the boat? Or could it be true that He still loves you when you do? I wouldn't be surprised if there are many times where you have to stop and regroup as you sift through the things you've been taught and the things you've experienced in order to reshape and reframe some of those old habits and patterns that have been holding you back for so long.

Imagine going on a hiking trip. You have your backpack all packed with everything you think you could possibly need and set out on the climb. As you make your way up the mountain, that backpack starts to get really heavy. You try to power through, but at some point, you have to stop. You slip the backpack off of your shoulders and unzip it. You sort through each of the items, determining if you really need them or not. The difference is that you're looking at them under a new light. At the bottom of the mountain, you were fine with shoving everything in there, just in case. But now, you know that you can't keep climbing unless you only bring what's essential and get rid of all of the fluff.

Our journey with Jesus is similar in a lot of ways. When we're just starting out, we have a tendency to pack every sermon, every piece of advice from a godly person, and every bit of theology into our bag. The difference is, if you're reading this book, you're most likely not a beginner anymore. Which means that since you've made it up the mountain a little ways, it's time to unpack that bag. Now, a lot of this will have to be done on your own. This is a journey between you and God, not you and me. John 16:13 says, "But when he, the Spirit of truth, comes, he will guide you into all the truth." That means that the Holy Spirit is not going to lead you in the wrong direction. Spoiler alert: I am not the Holy Spirit. My job is not to lead you the whole way. My job is to point you in the right direction so that He can. However, throughout this book, I will be unpacking my own bag for you, to give you an example of how this works. Because in order for you to know how to get up the rest of that mountain, it helps to have someone going ahead of you so that you can watch where they step.

Do I Have To?

Like I said before, this book is going to make you confront some uncomfortable things. It's really humbling to examine something you've believed for so long only to find out that it wasn't true the whole time. Sometimes, it's not even that they are untrue, they are just half truths that keep us from running at full speed. I'll give you an example. I used to believe that following Jesus was all about the rules. He's the boss, He's the captain, He's the drill sergeant. You don't question the drill sergeant. You just tell me what to do and I will do it, Sir.

That was, until the day when He asked me what I wanted out of life. I was flabbergasted. Befuddled, even. "You mean...I get to have a say?" Looking back now, it's almost comical, in a naive sort of way. We're told nearly every Sunday morning that God is our Father, and yet we never take the time to actually sit with that. What good, loving parent only barks out orders at their kids and never takes a breath to let their child give their opinion? If you think that's the kind of Father God is, there is so much more of His love for you to discover.

In Mark 10, we see Jesus walking along the road when a blind man named Bartimaeus calls out to Him. When He calls the man to Him, He asks the man, "What do you want me to do for you?" (Verse 51). I'm sure it was quite obvious to Jesus that this man was blind. But instead of Jesus telling Bartimaeus what he needed, or giving him a list of things to do in order to earn his vision, He asks him, "What do *you* want *me* to do *for you?*"

No, Jesus isn't the type to only tell us what we need to do, He's also the type to show us what's available to us by asking us what we want. I don't know about you, but I wish I had found that out a lot earlier. Yet, I had that heavy list of rules tucked away in my backpack, trying my hardest to climb that mountain without complaining. If only I had realized sooner that He only wanted to lighten my load. If only I had stopped looking under every rock and around every bush for some sort of instruction on what He wanted me to do. One thing I've learned since that day is this:

when you ask God for His opinion, He makes it known. If He has something specific He wants you to do, He'll show you. If He doesn't give you clear cut directions, sometimes it's because He's simply letting you choose. And you will only slow yourself down by looking so hard for instruction that you quit walking down the path.

Do you see where I'm going with this? If we don't confront the things that we've clung to for so long, we will never truly be able to discover if they were from God or not. We cannot chase the doctrine more than we chase the person. God is relational. He's not wanting you to memorize a bunch of facts about who people claim that He is, He's inviting you to come closer and see for yourself. Get to know Him on a personal level. Lighten your load. If you take the time to do that, you'll be surprised how much further you'll go.

This is one of those moments where we have to slow down to speed up. In fact, it seems that a lot of moments with God are like that. God gave me the idea for this book in July of 2024. I spent the next few months researching, making notes, and organizing information. By the time I sat down to write, I had myself wound so tightly that none of the words were coming out right. I was so stressed about saying everything correctly and making sure the messages were clear, not to mention finding the time to write with two children in tow. It became too overwhelming.

Until one day I just stopped. I pressed pause on the whole project. I went to God and said, "I cannot do this on my own. So I am going to spend a solid seven days getting back into alignment with you before I touch that computer again." Do you know what happened over those seven days? I did a whole lot of what the world would consider nothing. I did a puzzle, repotted my plants, played Barbies with my daughter and video games with my son. And I sat with God. And just through that simple act of resting and realigning, I was so filled up with a renewed fire and passion that I couldn't help but start writing. I was no longer trying to wring out every last bit of knowledge I had in me and hoping that it filled the pages of a book. Instead, it was coming from overflow.

Sometimes, stopping to reassess is not a bad thing. It's better to get your bearings and course correct now than it is to keep pushing yourself further and further down the wrong path, isn't it?

Expect the Unexpected

One of my favorite reality game shows to watch is Big Brother. There's just something fascinating to me about over a dozen people from different backgrounds with different personalities being crammed into one house together all while trying to navigate the social, mental, and physical aspects of the competition. However, each season comes with its own theme, twists, and challenges. Their motto is to "expect the unexpected." Why? Because it keeps the players on their toes. It keeps them from developing a formulaic way to win and gives everyone a fair shot at the cash prize.

While God is not a game show host that gets a kick out of watching you squirm when He throws you a curveball, He is guaranteed to keep you on your toes. The reason is because it helps us develop a certain level of dependency on Him in order to navigate the course ahead of us. God is a God of order and functionality, but that doesn't mean He's predictable. If you spend enough time with Him, you will see that He has no problem throwing your theology right out the window. Let's look at some biblical examples.

The first example that comes to mind is the story of Peter. Peter walked closely with Jesus throughout his ministry. He had even seen Jesus tell a Samaritan woman that He was sent to the Jews, and it wouldn't be right to take the children's bread and give it to the dogs (Matthew 15:26). And yet, after Jesus' ascension, Peter is minding his own business one day when God gives him a vision telling him to take the good news of the gospel to the Gentiles (Acts 10:9-16). Can you imagine how confusing that must've been for him? The whole time he was with Jesus, he's been thinking that this is for the Jews and Jews alone. And yet, now God is telling him something completely different.

This is why it's important to weigh everything in our bag, not only through scripture, but through personal experience with God. I promise you that if He is going to contradict something that you've always believed to be true, He will have scripture ready to back it up.

How about the Pharisees, who dedicated their whole lives to studying the scriptures? They seemed to be some of the only people Jesus had beef with because they constantly depended on their own interpretation of the scripture rather than cultivating a personal relationship with the author Himself. The thing is, we have got to learn to stop leaning on our own interpretation of scripture. Proverbs 3:5 says, "Trust in the Lord with all your heart, and lean not on your own understanding." We've all known people who have taken a scripture completely out of context and used it as a weapon to defend their own opinions. Maybe we've even been those people. The closer we get to understanding the Father's heart, the more easily we're able to spot whether or not something reflects Him.

The best way to interpret scripture is by developing a personal relationship with the Author. Think about it like having a tour guide at the zoo. If you're walking through the zoo, you can observe all of the animals and maybe even find out some interesting facts about them by reading the plaques in front of their enclosure. But if you have a tour guide leading you around the zoo, someone who is knowledgeable about the animals behavior, patterns, and the way they support and interact with nature itself, you'll have a far better understanding of those animals than you could ever have from observation alone. Remember that the Holy Spirit guides us into all truth. We can observe the Bible all we want. We can study it over and over again like the plaques at the zoo. But unless we are developing a relationship with the One who is intended to guide us, we won't ever have a deeper understanding.

What's Next?

Have you ever been working out and had an instructor or a trainer telling you not to stop moving? They don't really care if you're able to do the moves well, they just want to make sure that you keep your body moving. Why is that? It's because they know that if you stop, your chances of getting back up again are slim. They know that if you can make the decision to keep going even when things get hard, you'll be much more likely to develop the mental fortitude necessary to actually achieve your long term goals. But on the other hand, if you quit during the middle of your first few workouts, you'll probably quit before any of your hard work is reflected on the scale.

I've noticed the same pattern with people spiritually. Those who are quick to quit climbing when the mountain gets steep are the most likely to set up camp right where they are and never climb any further. But the ones who dig their heels in and don't give up are typically the ones God puts on the front lines, and for obvious reasons. You don't have to be a spiritual giant in order to be used by God, you just have to be determined not to quit.

By going through the process of unpacking our bag right now, you'll see how this sets us up for success on the road ahead. Remember that our spiritual journey is more like a marathon than a sprint. This idea is perfectly outlined for us in Hebrews 12:1 where it says, "Therefore, since we are surrounded by such a great cloud of witnesses, let us throw off everything that hinders and the sin that so easily entangles. And let us run with perseverance the race marked out for us." By removing everything that hinders us, it gives us a better chance to have the stamina and endurance necessary to not only finish the race, but finish it well.

I will say, though, that if you need to stop and unpack your bag multiple times throughout the journey, that's okay. In fact, I would encourage it. There's always the chance that we will miss something the first time. There will be plenty more times where we will feel weary along the journey. Whenever we reach these spiritual checkpoints, it's an indication that some adjustments need to be made in order for us to keep going. Stopping to take a break and reassess is not a sign of weakness, and it's not the same thing as quitting. Just make sure that when you need to rest, you set the intention to keep climbing. Although we're not setting out to reach some sort of spiritual peak, the whole point is for us to get closer to Jesus. To develop a deeper relationship with him. The "higher" you climb in this relationship, the lighter your load becomes. That's the heart of the Father. It's not about making sure you achieve something, it's about removing all of the baggage that weighs you down.

Chapter Three

Know Your Season

I'm just going to say it. Fairy tales have done us dirty. We've all grown up listening to stories that all sound the same. They have a sweet beginning, a rough middle, and a happy ending. Rinse and repeat. We love those stories. We *want* those stories. And so we convince ourselves that that's the way life should work. We think that if we have had a hard season of life, somehow we've earned the right to sit back and coast through the rest of life. Now, I want you to hear me when I say that our stories absolutely can have a happy ending, but this earth is not the ending. This earth is the brutal middle. Our lives here are where the messy character development part of the story takes place. So if you are somehow waiting for the point where you will reach your fairytale ending, I hate to break it to you, but as we say down here in the south, this ain't it.

I know, that was pretty harsh. I probably just burst your bubble. Shattered your hopes and dreams. Well, allow me to piece them back together. Because even though you may not get to the point where you've reached a happy ending here on earth, you *can* still get to a point where you actually enjoy your life. And you do that by learning to recognize your season. You see, each and every season of our lives is designed to serve a purpose. To teach us something, to mature us, to help us grow. And you can either run from it, or you can learn from it.

Did you know that cows and bison are essentially cousins in the animal kingdom? And although they share many similarities, there is one behavior pattern that sets them apart. See, when a storm is coming, cows tend to do one of two things. They either lay down, or they run away. Bison, on the other hand, run towards the storm. That may sound a little silly, but when you think about it, it's actually genius. By facing their problems head on, they have to endure the storm for a *much* shorter amount of time than their cousins. We all have a tendency to want to run away from our problems. We all want to lie down in the season that God has put us in and wait for it to pass. Because we often don't want to deal with the discomfort. What we don't realize is that comfort is the enemy of progress. If we would just turn and face it–if we would actually search for the lesson it's trying to teach us–we could get through it much faster, and gain more understanding along the way.

You know that old saying, "The grass is always greener on the other side"? Well, in this case, that's kind of true. By running away from the storms, what the cows are actually doing are running towards barren land that hasn't been watered. They're retreating to a place where all they will find is brown grass and dust to satisfy their hunger. On the other hand, the bison are running into lush pastures fresh with rain. They are pursuing fruitful ground. So, I guess the question is, which one sounds better to you? Are you ready to break free from this cycle you've been stuck in? Are you finally ready to be out of this storm that's persistently been chasing you down? Are you ready to see those green pastures that you've been dreaming of? Then it might just be time to stop, turn around, square your shoulders, and face this season head on.

Spiritual Maturity

One thing that plays a factor in the way you handle your season is your level of spiritual maturity. I think we can all agree that newborns are not capable of the same things that toddlers are. While a toddler can mostly get themselves dressed, even if their shoes are on the wrong feet, newborns rely solely on the care of others to meet their needs.

Maybe you're feeling a lot like a newborn right now. You've been in a place where you were warm, comfortable, and you didn't have to wait to get any of your needs met. Suddenly you've been thrust out of that place into a new environment that is absolutely assaulting your senses everywhere you turn. There's too many new things happening. Too much to adjust to. Before you came to know Jesus, your life seemed to be going pretty well. And now that you've decided to develop a relationship with him, all of a sudden, it feels like everything is out to get you. If that's you, chances are you're not going to be able to power through this season on your own. That may have been what you're used to, just pushing through in your own strength. But now, you're going to need a little extra help. You're going to need to cry out to your Father to get your needs met. But can I just encourage you for a second?

Although this is new and scary and hard, it is serving a massively important purpose. This season is meant to teach you how to rely on your Father. It's meant to teach you a holy dependence that will carry you through all of the seasons to come. If you grew up in a loving family, then you know that there are seasons of life that will stretch you and test you so much that all you want is your mama. It doesn't matter how old you are, how capable you are, how strong you are. Sometimes you just want your mama. Even if you didn't grow up in a loving household, you probably still have that same craving inside of you. Unfortunately, we don't always have that option. Sometimes our moms are gone too soon. Sometimes our moms were never there in the first place. But that craving remains.

The good news is that there is someone who can satisfy that desire. There's a reason why we crave that parental love and affection. It's because even before we belonged to an earthly family, we belonged to our heavenly Father. Jeremiah 1:5 says, "Before I formed you in the womb I knew you, before you were born I set you apart; I appointed you as a prophet to the nations." See, you may think that this season is hard, and you're right. But it's not because you're on your own. It's not because you're being punished for all of the less than perfect things you've done in your life. It's because your loving Father is drawing you back into his arms. He's putting you in situations that help you realize that this life was never designed for you to power through all by yourself. Trust me, this is the most loving thing he can do for you.

On the flip side, maybe you're not a newborn anymore. Maybe you've already walked through that season and you already know how to run back to your Father for comfort when you need it. You may have reached a point of maturity where you don't need your hand held quite as much. In those seasons, it's easy to feel like the grace has lifted off of your life. It's easy to become jealous of how easy it seems to be for everyone else. Like an older sibling welcoming a newborn in the family, you can start to wonder why some of God's other kids seem to be getting more attention than you. It can feel unfair, insensitive, and can even cause you to want to regress backwards so that maybe you can get back to that place of nurturing.

I remember feeling like that. I had just exited my "newborn season" and started to mature. All of a sudden, I missed that feeling of God's love coating me like a warm blanket. As hard as that newborn season was, there was a level of comfort attached to it that didn't seem to exist in this new place. I would see testimonies of people saying that a stranger bought their groceries, unprompted, or the exact amount of money they needed miraculously showed up in their bank account. I started to feel a bit jaded. "Hey God, I'm struggling too. Why don't you ever tell a stranger to buy my groceries?" And like any loving parent would, He gently replied, "Because that is for the people who are *learning* to trust me. You already know how to do that."

See, from my vantage point, it felt like I was being overlooked by God. Which opened an old wound that I didn't want to revisit. But even in this new space that I was beginning to explore, I started to see the purpose behind it. God was teaching me to trust myself. He was teaching me how to stand on my own two feet, while still reaching for his hand to steady me. I was maturing. This was the whole point. It's easy to lose sight of that in the moment if you don't know your season.

It's also easy to get a little "big for your britches" as my grandmother would say. Meaning, as you mature, you can reach a point where you feel like you know a lot more than you actually do. Once toddlers hit a certain age, it seems like they all have the same favorite sentence. "I can do it myself." They think that because they have matured a little bit, they suddenly don't need help anymore. That is, until they fall flat on their face, spill their juice, or get stuck inside the shirt they were trying to take off. Honestly, this isn't unique to toddlers. Teenagers can be the same way. I remember when I turned eighteen. Man, I thought I knew everything. See, I was aware of the fact that I wasn't a child anymore, but I wasn't aware of how much I didn't know about being an adult in the real world. A few years later, I wasn't so quick to brag about how much I knew because reality had finally set in.

Humility comes in handy right about now. Because in order to handle this season of life well, you have to learn how to walk in humility. If you strut around thinking you can't possibly learn anything new or that you have somehow "arrived" at a level of spiritual maturity, you're going to need to humble yourself before life experience does it for you. Ask me how I know. This is the point where you recognize that no matter how much you know, there is always more to learn.

The whole point is that spiritually maturing is the goal. Just like in the physical world, we aren't meant to stay spiritual babies forever. The only difference between the physical and spiritual realm is that spiritually maturing is a choice. You get to decide if you want to move past this stage or not. So if you want to mature, if you want to unlock all of the potential that God has set before you, you're going to have to not only recognize your season, but walk it out.

The Four Seasons

Fall is by far my favorite season of the year. I absolutely *live for* the colors of the leaves changing, the crisp wind that's not too cool, the sweaters, the hot chocolate, the bonfires, the beanies, Gilmore girls on repeat and *all* of the seasonal candles–yes, all of them. In fact, I love the fall so much that I often find myself wishing we could just hurry up and get the other seasons over with. Sure, I'll enjoy the flowers in the spring and the beach and lake days in the summer, but I very rarely allow myself to enjoy the *whole* season.

Come on, admit it. You do that too, don't you? You're so ready to get to the good part that you wish away all of the less desirable stuff, even though you know it serves a purpose. We know that all four of the seasons are necessary to sustain the cycle of life, yet we all want to rush the seasons. I'm convinced it's human nature. But if you really want to get to the point where you can fully enjoy your life–where you can *thrive*–you don't need a change of season, you need a change of perspective.

In Acts 16, we see the story of Paul and Silas stuck in prison. This is what verse 25 says, "About midnight Paul and Silas were praying and singing hymns to God, and the other prisoners were listening to them." Hold on. Pause. These men were in prison. Not only that, they had just been beaten half to death, and as if that weren't enough, they had their feet put in stocks. And yet–*they're singing?*

Be honest. Could you ever imagine yourself getting to that point? Do you ever think you would be singing and praising God when you're going through one of the toughest seasons of your life? Would you laugh at me if I told you that you could get to that point, too? Because it's true. Paul wasn't built differently than you. God didn't give him an extra dose of courage or strength or determination than He gave you. You have all of the same tools in your tool belt that Paul had. Do you want to know how I know? Because Paul had two key pieces that helped him withstand some of the wildest storms. He had The Holy Spirit, and he had understanding. If you're reading this book, I'm assuming that you've already accepted Jesus' sacrifice on the cross, meaning you already have The Holy Spirit living inside of you. Now, let me help with the second one.

James 1:2-4, "Consider it pure joy, my brothers and sisters, whenever you face trials of many kinds, because you know that the testing of your faith produces perseverance. Let perseverance finish its work so that you may be mature and complete, not lacking anything." You see, Paul understood how seasons worked. He understood that God would not put you through anything without the intent of it bringing something amazing out of you. He understood that if he was going through something difficult, it meant that he was about to learn something incredible through it. If life was going smoothly, that peace was counted as a win. But when the struggles came, he valued the lesson he would learn more than the trouble he would go through. It was a win. Either way, he couldn't lose. And the more difficult the struggle, the greater the maturity on the other side. Paul wasn't shying away from the storms, he was embracing them.

When I was a kid, there was this cartoon movie that sort of became an unconventional classic. It was called *The Emperor's New Groove*. The whole plot is about this prideful Emperor named Kuzco living a cushy lifestyle. At first, he's rude, obnoxious, and insanely arrogant. One day, his ex-advisor decides to poison him and take the throne for herself. Except, instead of killing him, she accidentally turns him into a llama. Overnight, his whole kingdom is torn away from him. But as he moves through the journey back to the palace, he is faced with challenge after challenge that humbles him and turns him into the kind of Emperor who is deserving of the throne.

There's one scene in particular that always cracks me up. Kuzco and his friend, Pacha, are bound to a log that is floating down a rushing river. Kuzco is looking upstream, unable to see what lies ahead of him. At one point he hears Pacha say, "Uh-oh." His response is, "Don't tell me. We're headed for a huge waterfall? Sharp rocks at the bottom?" When Pacha confirms the direness of the situation, Kuzco's eyes narrow as he says, "Bring it on." Do you want to know what's funny about this scene? That waterfall led to them being freed from the very thing they were bound to. It allowed them to get a step further on their journey. If they had fought against it, tried to flail and kick their way to safety, it would've been no use. In fact, it may have gotten them hurt even further.

Paul understood this attitude. Prison? Bring it on. Shipwreck? Bring it on. Snake bite? Bring it on. It didn't matter what you threw at him, he was determined to see it through. Why? Because he knew it would make him more like Jesus. He knew it would remove everything that was holding him back so that he would become more like the person he loved and admired the most. And becoming more like Jesus means that life may not be any easier, but you're able to see the bigger picture. Mentally, the load becomes a lot lighter and a lot more meaningful when you see that all of your suffering serves a greater purpose.

Did you know that trees still grow in the winter?[1] You wouldn't think so, because they look dead. All of their leaves have fallen off. They seem to lie dormant, like statues whose only purpose seems to be a reminder of what was. But even in that dormant

---

1. Arbor Day Foundation, on tree growth and dormancy in winter.

winter season, the tree is growing in a new way. You see, it may not be putting out new leaves or stretching its branches, but under the surface, those roots are expanding in ways they never have before. This underground growth is preparing the tree for the next season.

I want you to hear me in this. Lean in, because it's important that you understand what I'm about to say. Whatever you're going through right now is meant to equip you for the season that is to come. We all want the shiny gifts. We all want the Promised Land. But the whole point of the wilderness was to strip the Israelites of the mindsets they developed in Egypt so that when they got to the Promised Land, they could actually enjoy it and steward it well. The things you are going through right now are giving you the tools you need to steward the promises to come. But you have to lean into it. See, most of the Israelites didn't make it out of that wilderness. They fought and kicked and bucked so hard against God that he finally let them have what they thought they wanted. They continued to hold onto their old mindset of acting like slaves, rather than switching into a mindset of being children of God. Only a handful of people understood the assignment. Don't miss the lesson in this season, friend. It could be the very thing that leads you to your destiny.

Pruning Season

Do you want to hear something hilarious? Most of the time, when people meet me and get to know me, they compliment me on how calm I am, how unshakeable and steady I seem to be. And, truthfully, I am not phased by a whole lot. But I wasn't always that way. If you had met me pre-2020, you'd think you were looking at an entirely different person. I was rigidity personified. If plans changed unexpectedly, it would upset my apple cart and send me into a tailspin. To put it plainly, I was *not* good at rolling with the punches.

So what changed? Well, you might not like the answer. What changed was that I had so many punches thrown at me, that I learned how to cowboy up. In my first book,[2] I shared the story of how my dad was diagnosed with cancer in 2020 and that same week, God asked me to have another baby. If you read that book, you know that I said yes to that insanely scary request, despite the fact that I was quaking in my boots the whole time. I can remember looking down at my swollen belly one day as I was praying for our daughter. God spoke to me so clearly in that moment and said, "She is going to make you adaptable."

Uh-oh. Typically, when you're praying for your kids, you want to hear God tell you how sweet and gentle and loving they will be. But making me *adaptable?* Oh boy, I knew I was baking a little firecracker at that moment. It's part of the reason why we gave her a name that means "fair warrior." Because she is just that.

I was always told that the second childbirth is much quicker than the first. Not in my case. Both of my labors were 27.5 hours long, almost to the minute. Do you want to know why? Because

---

2. *7 Days to a Life of Limitless*

when I am in extreme pain, I have a natural tendency to clamp down on that pain. I grit my teeth, and clench all of my muscles until the pain subsides. Well, apparently I'm a lot stronger than I thought I was, because I was completely unaware that clamping down on my pain was what was holding my babies in my body longer than they should have been. Everyone told me that you are supposed to breathe through the contractions. I don't remember ever being taught to relax through them. So I didn't. I fought them, for as long and as hard as I could until all of my strength left me and I had no choice but to just let it happen.

Whenever we fight against the pain that God is allowing to take place in our lives, we are delaying the very thing that he is trying to birth through us. Hear me when I say this: there is always a blessing on the other side of your pain. Most people just don't stick with it long enough to figure that out. If you want to experience the birth of new things in your life, most of the time, you're going to have to go through the painful parts of labor.

Just when I thought the hard part was over, the hits kept coming. Little did I know God was walking me through a whole season of pruning me of the old mindsets that had been holding me back. A week after I gave birth to her, I noticed a pretty intense stomach pain that seemed to be lingering longer than any of the other postpartum pains. I went back to my doctor who confirmed that during childbirth, I had pushed so hard to get her out that I had herniated a muscle in my upper abdomen. She said, "If you don't want to have to correct this with surgery, I suggest you rest as much as possible." So I went home and did just that. Little did

I know that I had already contracted Covid-19. So all of that rest I was doing was just allowing the virus to fester inside my lungs, turning into Covid Pneumonia.

Two weeks after giving birth, I was admitted back into the hospital with Covid Pneumonia during a time where visitors were strictly prohibited. I had to leave my exclusively breastfed baby in the hands of my husband, who wasn't given the opportunity to say goodbye to me before I was locked inside of the hospital for five days. I spent those five days in a windowless exam room on the Emergency Room floor, listening to people code outside my door every few hours. My oxygen levels were dangerously low. At the time I was admitted, my oxygen was down to 82. My mom (who is a physician's assistant) later informed me that that is the point when organ failure begins and some people have to be put on a ventilator.

For those five days, I never saw the sun, and I only saw another human being every four hours when the nurses came to check my vitals and administer my breathing treatments. I was so dehydrated that my veins were blown out twice when they tried to attach my I.V. and when they finally got a vein, it was at an angle that didn't allow me to bend my elbow at all. In order to go to the bathroom, I would have to take off my oxygen, wheel my I.V. pole down the hall to the only bathroom, and clean myself up with my one arm that I could use. I was only two weeks postpartum, remember? Use your imagination. I had to do all of this in the hopes that I wouldn't pass out before I could make it back to my room and reattach my oxygen.

And yet, the whole time I was in the hospital, all I could think about was my newborn daughter. Of course, I thought about my whole family, but I knew my baby girl's survival was borderline dependent on me getting out of there alive. Of course, she *could* have made it without me. My husband could have raised her whether I was able to pull through or not, but she wouldn't have what she needed to thrive. She wouldn't have had the best start to life that I could give her if I had chosen to give up at that point.

That hospital stay was one of the most pivotal times of my life. Because God was right, my baby girl made me adaptable. She gave me a reason to push through the hard stuff to get to the other side. It wasn't easy. Come on, my body was literally shutting down. Do you think that's an easy thing to overcome? Do you think it was easy to listen to all of the people dying right outside my door? It was one of the hardest things I've ever done in my life. But God gave me the hope I needed to keep going, and I have no doubt he will do the same for you.

1 Corinthians 10:13 says, "No temptation has overtaken you except what is common to mankind. And God is faithful; he will not let you be tempted beyond what you can bear. But when you are tempted, he will also provide a way out so that you can endure it." When you are tempted to give up, tempted to throw in the towel, tempted to lay down and die, God will give you everything you need to keep going. But here's the kicker, you have to take it. You cannot reject the help God sends you. You cannot pray to be rescued and refuse to grab onto the life raft. However, when we are in those seasons, it's easy to miss. It's so easy to get lost in

the grief of our circumstances that we struggle to see what God is doing. If you find yourself in a season like this, my advice to you is simple: look for the way out. God is faithful to provide one.

Chapter Four

Implied Victory

I won't lie to you; I almost didn't finish this book. As I was writing it, I was walking through a season in life where I felt defeated. I wasn't sure how I was supposed to encourage people through their storms if I couldn't seem to manage my own. During all of this, I was doing everything that God had already taught me in past seasons. I was shifting my mindset to look for the lessons that He was teaching me through those hard times. I was asking for help and encouragement when I needed it. I was surrounded with an amazing group of people who took the time to pour into me and encourage me and guide me through the thick of it. I knew that I had done everything I could possibly do. And yet, it didn't seem to make much of a difference. Something was still missing.

As I prayed about it one day, I told God, "I know that I did everything that I possibly could. I can see the lessons you wanted me to learn. I have felt encouraged and supported, so why do I still feel empty? God, I need you to reveal something to me that has some real weight behind it. I need the kind of encouragement that not only helps me get up again, but that helps me to come up swinging." Boy, did He deliver.

Go to the Enemy's Camp

After I said that prayer, God led me to the story of Gideon. If anyone understands what it's like to be defeated, it's Gideon. When we are first introduced to him in Judges 6, he's so oppressed and discouraged that he is hiding his food so that the Midianites don't steal it from him. The Midianites had been tormenting the people of Israel for seven years at this point. And there was nothing Gideon could do about it. At least, not without God's help. Not only was he the least in his family, but his family was the weakest clan in his tribe. He found himself in a situation that felt completely and utterly hopeless, and all he could do was try to survive it. Then one day, the angel of the Lord appears to him and tells him that he's going to rescue his entire nation from this oppression. Gideon responded in the same way that I probably would have. He listed all of the reasons why he had every right to be discouraged. And yet, that didn't stop God.

Over the next chapter, we see opportunities and situations being used to build Gideon's confidence in God. Fast forward a little bit and you'll see that Gideon is finally ready to go to battle. He has accumulated an army of 32,000 men that are ready to follow him into the Midianite camp and finish this thing once and for all. But just as they are about to set out, God shakes things up.

Through the process of elimination, he completely strips Gideon of his army until only 300 men remain with him.

It's at this point that I imagine Gideon felt a lot like I had felt when I was going through this last season of my life. I had been walking with God. I had seen him come through and confirm His Word time and time again. I had gained confidence in God, confidence in myself, and favor with others. And then that confidence was shaken. All of a sudden, it felt like I was going backwards. Like I was losing ground. And I couldn't see my way to victory from there. That must've been how Gideon felt. He had finally amassed this massive army that was going to help him carry out what God had called him to do, and then in the blink of an eye, it was gone. Nevertheless, God hadn't changed His mind. He called Gideon to keep walking forward anyway. And what He told Gideon next is what really rocked my world.

In Judges 7:9-11, we see God telling Gideon exactly what was going to happen. Take a look. "During that night the Lord said to Gideon, 'Get up, go down against the camp, because I am going to give it into your hands. If you are afraid to attack, go down to the camp with your servant Purah and listen to what they are saying. Afterward, you will be encouraged to attack the camp.' So he and Purah his servant went down to the outposts of the camp." At this point, God gives Gideon the implied victory. But that's not really anything new. God had been telling him that he was going to defeat the Midianites from the first time he appeared to Gideon. This time, He gave Gideon a different strategy. He told him to go listen to what the enemy was saying, and that would give him the encouragement he needed to rise up and fight. What could the enemy possibly have to say that would cause Gideon to rise up and attack an entire army that has been oppressing them for seven years with only 300 men in tow? Let's skip down to verses 13-15 to find out.

Here's what it says, "Gideon arrived just as a man was telling a friend his dream. 'I had a dream,' he was saying. 'A round loaf of barley bread came tumbling into the Midianite camp. It struck the tent with such force that the tent overturned and collapsed.' His friend responded, 'This can be nothing other than the sword of Gideon son of Joash, the Israelite. God has given the Midianites and the whole camp into his hands.' When Gideon heard the dream and its interpretation, he bowed down and worshiped. He returned to the camp of Israel and called out, 'Get up! The Lord has given the Midianite camp into your hands.'" Do you see what a drastic difference there is in Gideon's confidence level here? He goes from feeling defeated and discouraged, to receiving the kind of encouragement that caused him to come up swinging. If you read the rest of the story, you'll see that Gideon was able to defeat the Midianites without ever removing his sword from its sheath. The Midianite army was so terrified that when the horns blew, they all turned and attacked each other.

So what was so significant about that dream that caused such a drastic shift for Gideon? Here's my theory. Gideon knew that God was on his side. He even knew that God was capable of defeating the Midianites. The problem was that Gideon didn't believe in himself. His fear probably stemmed from the feeling that he was capable of messing it all up. Honestly, I've been there. At one point or another, I think we all have. We've all felt a little incapable of the things that God has called us to. And sometimes, we even feel incapable of the basics of trusting God without fear or doubt. What changed it all for Gideon wasn't another sign or confirmation. That wasn't what solidified his belief that God really did see him as a mighty warrior. What solidified his belief was eavesdropping on the enemy.

It's one thing for our friends and family to encourage us. Most of the time, they want the best for us. They want to see us win. Sometimes it's even hard to latch onto what God says about us. The reason why this dream was so encouraging was because Gideon discovered that his enemies believed in his victory more than he did. This information was coming from someone who had no incentive to want him to win. They were his enemies. They were fighting against him. They *wanted* to defeat him. And yet, even they believed in the victory that was already implied. If we truly want the kind of encouragement that causes us to rise to our feet ready to fight, it might benefit us to take a page from Gideon's playbook and listen in on what the enemy is saying about us.

Now, I want you to hear what I'm saying. I know you've been told your whole life not to listen to the voice of the enemy. And in some ways, that's true. You should never listen to what the enemy says...to your face. But what he's saying when he thinks you're not listening? That's a completely different story. Yes, to your face, the enemy will always try to discourage you. He will try to taunt you, to confuse you, to convince you that you can't win. But behind your back? He believes in your victory more than you do.

Think about it. Why would the enemy try to convince you to be fearful? It's because he knows exactly what will happen to him if that fear is removed and you step into your calling. Why would he try to convince you to feel sorry for yourself? Because he knows what will happen to him if you're no longer distracted by your circumstances. He knows that your victory is already implied. That God has already decided that you're going to beat this. So the best chance he's got is to try and convince you otherwise. It's his only move. But once you can pinpoint why he's trying so hard to stop you, you will receive that same encouragement needed to rise up and fight back.

Strengthen Yourself in the Lord

You know who else was well acquainted with the feeling of defeat? King David. Most of the time, when we think of David, we reflect on all of his victories. How he was anointed to be king. How he defeated the lion, the bear, and ultimately Goliath. How he overcame every single thing that was thrown at him. We often skip over the part of his life that highlights all of the times he felt defeated. We flip through the pages that talk about when he felt broken, betrayed, and confused. But I think there's a valuable lesson we can learn from David during those times.

There's one story in particular that stands out to me. Let me set the scene for you. It all starts in 1 Samuel 29. Here's what's happening. David has been on the run from King Saul, his father-in-law, who has quite literally tried to kill him multiple times. And you thought your family was crazy. While he's on the run, David decides to run to the last place he thinks Saul will check. Enemy territory. But during his time in the enemy camp, David starts to do what we all do when we are entertaining the enemy for too long. He started to conform to those patterns. So much so that he wanted to join their army and fight with the Philistines *against* Israel. Talk about a drastic turn of events. And the Philistines almost let him follow through with it, too. Ultimately, the other kings got suspicious of where David's allegiance lied and they thought it would be best not to trust him. So the Philistine king sends David and his men back to Ziklag, where they had been living while they had been on the run from Saul.

Here's where things get dicey. When David and his men return to Ziklag, they find their homes and all of their possessions burned to the ground. Every member of their family had been kidnapped in the process. David's men were so heartbroken that they were tempted to turn on David and stone him on the spot.

Let's pause right here for a minute. I want you to think about how David must have felt. He's been fighting for his life for years, doing whatever it took to survive all of the circumstances that had been thrown at him. And it's all led to this. Not only has he lost everything he cared about, but now his friends who have been with him for years all decide to turn on him at once. Think about that level of betrayal. Of heartbreak. I'm sure on some level you can relate to David. You may not have lost literally everything and everyone you've cared about, but I'd be willing to bet you understand that feeling of hopelessness. I'll bet you know what it feels like to not be able to see your way out of whatever it is that you're going through. The good news is that the Bible gives us solutions to these problems. It's like a roadmap to show us what to do next when we don't know where to go. Let's use that map to get you out of here, shall we?

Take a look at what David does next. 1 Samuel 30:6 says, "David was greatly distressed because the men were talking of stoning him; each one was bitter in spirit because of his sons and daughters. But David found strength in the Lord his God." See there? David found strength in the Lord. That was what brought him out of distress. That was what gave him the courage to keep going. You may be thinking, *Great advice, but what does that even mean? How do you even go about strengthening yourself in the Lord?* That's a great question. Let's keep reading to find out.

Verse 7 and 8 say, "Then David said to Abiathar the priest, the son of Ahimelek, 'Bring me the ephod.' Abiathar brought it to him, and David inquired of the Lord, 'Shall I pursue this raiding party? Will I overtake them?' 'Pursue them,' he answered. 'You will certainly overtake them and succeed in the rescue.'" There it is. David strengthened himself in the Lord by asking the questions some of us are too afraid to ask out loud. God, should I even continue? Is it even worth it to keep going? If I do keep going, will it even be worth it, or will I keep tasting defeat after defeat?

In that moment, God answered his cry for help with a sign of hope. An implied victory. Not only did he tell David to keep going, He told David that if he did keep going, he would win. Sometimes that's all we need to keep pushing through the hard times. All we need is to know that it won't be like this forever. That there is a light at the end of this tunnel. That there is a God who sees us and wants good things for us. You may not be in a position where you feel like you have that same level of reassurance right now, but you already do.

My favorite verse in the Bible is Romans 8:28. "And we know that in all things God works for the good of those who love him, who have been called according to his purpose." If you love God, and if you are doing your best to follow him, your victory is already implied. Not because of anything you're doing or not doing, but because you have a loving Father who has your best interests at heart. I'm sure you've heard the saying "If it's not good, God's not done." To me, that's exactly what that verse means. I don't know about you, but I'm not willing to walk out on this story until I get to the good part.

Sometimes strengthening yourself in the Lord just means that you are clinging to the promises that are already given to you in that love letter (Bible) sitting on your nightstand. David understood this when he wrote Psalm 27. In verse 13, David says, "I remain confident of this: I will see the goodness of the Lord in the land of the living." The problem is that most of us want a quick fix. We have a tendency to think that if God is all powerful, it means He should come through for us when and where and how we want Him to. But what we will see throughout this book is that God is far more concerned with using our struggles to strengthen and refine us than he is about giving us a comfortable life.

Seeing with Spiritual Eyes

Stepping into victory requires a shift in perspective. We cannot achieve spiritual victory by looking at our circumstances through natural eyes. In order for us to actually believe we can win, we have to look at the situation from a different perspective. From God's perspective.

In 2 Kings, there is a story about the King of Aram trying to capture Elisha. The king finds out where Elisha is staying and sends an entire army with horses and chariots to surround the city. Elisha's servant sees all of this happening and feels defeated. But even though he was completely surrounded, Elisha didn't panic. Instead, look at what happens in verses 15-17. "When the servant of the man of God got up and went out early the next morning, an army with horses and chariots had surrounded the city. 'Oh no, my lord! What shall we do?' the servant asked. 'Don't be afraid,' the prophet answered. 'Those who are with us are more than those who are with them.' And Elisha prayed, 'Open his eyes, Lord, so that he may see.' Then the Lord opened the servant's eyes, and he looked and saw the hills full of horses and chariots of fire all around Elisha."

The servant was looking at the situation with natural eyes. He saw what a pickle they were in. He felt the gravity of the situation. The thing is, Elisha did too. But that wasn't *all* he saw. He also saw what God was doing in the midst of it. He could see God's hand moving behind the scenes. He saw with spiritual eyes. And when he prayed that his servants eyes would be opened, the servants perspective was drastically changed. He was no longer panicked or defeated. Even though he still didn't know for certain how things were going to play out, he saw that because God was with them, the odds were tilted in their favor.

Sometimes all it takes to get out of this place of feeling defeated is simply remembering that God is with us, that He is for us, and that He has already promised to make it alright in the end. Sometimes all it takes is remembering that your Father truly does love you.

I remember a specific situation where God taught me to see with spiritual eyes. We used to have a horse named Buddy. I had prayed for a horse since I was seven years old. Then one day, out of the blue, we were given this Welsh pony. I didn't care that he was old. I didn't care that I couldn't ride him because his back was too weak to support my weight. In my mind, this animal was an answered prayer. He has since passed away due to old age, but for the year and a half that we had him, Buddy taught me so much about healing and great faith and God's love. I never would've learned those lessons without him and I truly do not regret a single moment I had with him, even as chaotic as it was.

A few months after we got Buddy, he had a choking incident. Buddy loved food and had a habit of eating way too quickly. On this particular day, guzzling his food down too fast made it all get stuck in his throat. I'm not sure how much you know about horses, but choking for them isn't as big of an emergency as it is for humans. When humans choke, we can't breathe and we will die within minutes. But because horse's windpipes are in a separate place, they can choke for quite a while. When I noticed he was choking, I did all of my research to try and figure out what to do.

From what I could gather, most choking incidents can resolve themselves within a few hours, after that, veterinary intervention is needed. When Buddy's situation didn't resolve itself, we called the equine vet to make a house call. The vet tried to siphon the food out of his throat by pouring water down a tube that he had fished up his nose. Yes, it was as gross and traumatic as it sounds. After half an hour, the vet let us know that there was nothing he could do. Something was causing a blockage. Our only hope was to either put him down, or to take him in for emergency surgery an hour away once that clinic reopened after the weekend, if he could make it that long.

Call me crazy (many people have) but I wasn't ready to give up on Buddy just yet. We decided not to have him put down immediately because I wanted to make sure I took the time to really pray about it before I made a decision based on sheer emotion and adrenaline. From that point, Buddy's condition progressively worsened. At one point, my husband looked at me and said, "Babe, we might have to put him down. We can't just let him suffer." I knew he was right. But I also knew there was something God was teaching me through it. I said, "I know I don't get to determine what happens, but what I do know is that God sets up shop in the impossible. So I know that He's with us even through this." I truly didn't know what was going to happen to Buddy. I was not fully convinced that the situation would turn out how I wanted it to. But I was fully convinced that God had my back. I had seen him show up in my life too many times in much worse situations. So I knew that whatever happened, He was going to walk me through it one step at a time.

The next day, Buddy was miraculously healed. We found him down by the pond chugging water as if nothing had ever happened. I'm not saying that what I did was a formula for a miracle. There have been times where I've seen miracles and times where I've not been spared from tragedy. What I am saying is that seeing that situation from a spiritual perspective changed things for me. It helped me to realize that even though I was scared to death of my circumstances, I knew that no matter which way you sliced it, I was going to come out of this braver, stronger, and with more understanding than I had before. Either way I was going to win. Either way, the weapon that had been formed against me was not going to prosper.

Victory isn't about getting the outcome you desire. It's about realizing that your winning is not dependent on the outcome, it's dependent on who your God is. Sometimes we just have to have the strength to recognize that He's already won, so our victory is already implied.

Chapter Five

Insecurity

Okay, friend. This is where we get into the real meaty stuff. Hopefully, I've done enough to convince you to pursue everything God has for your life, no matter how much risk may be involved. So this is the part where I go first. Over the next few chapters, I'm going to be taking out each of the skeletons in my closet, one by one. The whole purpose of this is to show you that I'm not asking you to do anything I wouldn't be willing to do. I'm not asking you to confront something that I myself wouldn't be willing to confront. Fair warning, though. This is going to get pretty heavy. It's okay if you need to take a minute to process the different chapters before moving on. But I think if you stick with it until the end, you'll wind up leaving with more hope than you had before you started.

For the sake of this story, I need to take a minute to give you some context. Let's start from the beginning, shall we? I'm the middle child and eldest daughter in a very loving, very well-intentioned family. My parents provided us with the best life they possibly could. But even the best of families can't protect a child from the cruelties of the world. It wasn't long before people started to point out my differences. Most of the time, they weren't rude about it. They would just kind of cock their heads to the side and say things like "You're not like the other two are you?" or "How come you don't play sports like your siblings?" It wasn't long before I concluded that "different" equals "not good enough." Different means you fall short of the standard, or so I thought.

At home, I was a happy, goofy kid. My mom has scrapbooks full of pictures of me doing some pretty quirky things. If you'd ask her, I'd bet she'd say that her favorite is the picture of me at two years old in my corduroy overalls wearing a plastic construction hat on my head and a sock on one foot with the other sock hanging out of my mouth, walking around the house as if nothing was amiss. My family loved my quirkiness. I got it from my dad. It kept my mom in stitches and provided endless entertainment for my siblings. But once people started to make those subtle comments, it led me to believe that maybe my goofy personality was best left inside the home.

As I grew older, I picked up on the faces people would make when I would crack a joke that they didn't quite understand or recite a movie quote out of context. Suddenly the word "goofy" was being substituted for words like "weird." The longer this went on, the more reserved I became. I still had friends that I would hang out with, and I quickly learned how to alter my personality to suit their individual preferences. If they liked a part of my personality, I would share it with them. The parts they didn't like, however, got tucked away for home. I developed quite a knack for reading people, but I never did understand why certain parts of me seemed to be so off-limits.

Does any of this sound familiar? Maybe you dealt with the same issues I had. Maybe the words spoken over you or the messages you picked up on were completely different. The fact of the matter is, we all do this. I don't care how well-adjusted or confident someone seems. At some point in their life, I can guarantee you they have been insecure about something. And most of the time, it's something they've been carrying around since they were a child. Just like I was.

All of those subtle comments and unsuspecting whispers came to a head one day when I was in upper elementary. This was the day that I came to learn just how "wrong" my true identity was. Isn't it wild how one statement or one situation can cause us to form deep, core beliefs about who we are? The encounters that we have seem to shape the fabric of our identity. If an idea enters our mind one too many times, it starts to become our reality. That's exactly what happened to me that day.

My mom had to work late, so she had asked the mom of a friend of mine if it would be alright if I rode home from school with them and stayed there until she was able to pick me up. My friend's mom agreed. As I jumped into their car that day, I noticed just how quiet it was. I was never the one to utter the first word. That would mean that I had to forfeit my advantage on reading the room and I wasn't about to do that. I thought to myself that they must be a quiet family, which made me very uncomfortable. I much preferred being around noisier people who would allow me to shrink into the sofa cushions and not think twice about it. When we arrived at their house, the mom led us into her bedroom where she sat me on the bench at the foot of her bed. She handed me a remote control, gestured to the TV and said, "Watch whatever you want. We're going shopping. Don't move until we get back." I locked eyes with her disapproving look and sheepishly nodded my head before looking away. Not another word was said. Out the door they went.

I'm not sure how much time went by before my friend's dad walked in. He froze as if there were a pint-sized robber in his home, with the only intention of squatting in front of their TV. We had never officially met before and I'm not sure he had any clue who I was. My suspicion was confirmed when he said, "Uhh....who are you?" I stuttered and stumbled over my words as I blurted out, "I'm Caitlin. I go to school with your daughter. They brought me home today." Still with a confused look on his face, he followed up with the question, "And where are they?" "They went shopping," I replied. Suddenly his face shifted from confusion to anger as he said through gritted teeth, "And they *left you here*?!" Again, all I could muster was a barely visible nod as he stormed out of the room, cell phone already in hand.

When my friend and her mom came back, they hardly spoke another word to me. The mom was seething with anger that seemed to be pointed in my direction. I spent the rest of the afternoon trying to quite literally bury myself in my homework before my mom came to pick me up. I told her everything that happened and needless to say, that was the last time I ever went back to that house.

Now, I know that this is drastically less significant than many people's childhood struggles. All in all, I had a good life. But that didn't change the fact that something inside of me broke that day. I knew that kids were brutally honest and wouldn't always like you, but I never expected it from an adult who, to the best of my knowledge, I had been nothing but kind to. *People just don't like you.* That was the lie that transitioned from an occasional thought to a core belief within one afternoon. From that point on, I struggled to make friends. I struggled to keep friends. I was riddled with anxiety if I even smelled the whiff of rejection lingering in the air. And it was something I thought I would have to live with for the rest of my life.

As time went on, I trusted myself less and less. Being myself seemed to be the very thing that got me bullied, ridiculed, or rejected so how could I trust myself to make any kind of decisions? I constantly felt as though I needed someone else to come in and save me, to tell me what to do, to make me better. Jesus seemed like the perfect solution. If only I could get Him close enough to fix me without seeing all of the really tragic parts of my identity, everything would work out. Little did I know, He didn't want to fix me. He wanted to restore me.

During one of my conversations with God, I remember Him saying to me, "We are not working towards the best version of you. We are working towards getting back to the person you've always been." The situations we find ourselves in seem to mold our identity and turn us into people that we never were before. People who are afraid, lonely, broken, sick and maybe want to give up altogether. But that's not who He created us to be.

Because I let that woman tell me who I was (even without her saying a word), I began to live a life of defeat. But that's not the destiny God has in mind for me, or anyone else for that matter. Do you remember King David? How he was anointed as king and then became a vagabond and a renegade before finally returning to take his rightful place on the throne? Much like David, I deserted my true identity. I let that opposition define me and grow roots within me. But, just like David, I eventually found my way back. And if you're living life from a defeated place, running from your true identity because the opposition seems too difficult to face, I'd love to help you find your way back too.

Here's the thing. I don't like to "victim shame." It's not really my style. I don't see any benefit of telling someone who has experienced something horrible at the hands of another human that they can just fix it. That's not at all what I'm trying to do. I understand better than anyone what it's like to go through hell and back because someone chose to treat me poorly. Believe me, that story I shared with you is not the worst one in my collection, not by a long shot. So I don't want you to feel like I'm trying to slap a bandaid on your bullet wound. What I am trying to do is empower you. I want to acknowledge your pain in all of its depth and then tell you that you don't have to stay there any longer. I want to give you a hand to help you up out of that pit you've been trapped in for far too long. Because I've been in the very pit you're sitting in and I found a way out. So if you're fed up with this pain, if you want to kick the spirit of defeat right in the teeth and claw your way out of here, I'd be more than happy to show you the path I took. It's just going to require us to face some of the hardest stuff first.

Insecurity Steals Your Identity

There's always going to be someone that you perceive to be better than you. Someone more attractive, more gifted, more capable. And if the only thing you're focused on is what seems to be missing from your life, you've fallen right into the enemy's trap. You do realize that you have a choice in what you focus on, don't you? Yes, our minds all have tendencies to drift in a certain direction, but that doesn't mean you have to allow it.

Have you ever driven a car that is in bad need of realignment? Whenever your car needs an alignment, you'll likely be able to tell because the steering wheel will seem to pull in one direction or another without your consent. So what do you do? Do you just let the car go off the road because that seems to be the natural direction it's headed in? No! You have a steering wheel in your hands for a reason. You use it to direct that car wherever it's supposed to go.

Your mind is the same way. Just because it naturally drifts towards insecurity doesn't mean that you can't take those thoughts captive and make them obedient to Christ (2 Corinthians 10:5). Yes, Jesus is the one giving you direction, but it's up to you to use the steering wheel that's in your hands to follow that direction. And if you notice that those thoughts are tugging at the wheel, making it difficult to steer, maybe it's time to get an alignment. Get into the Word and study what the Bible has to say about those thoughts. The more in alignment you are with your true identity, the easier it will be to steer in the right direction with little resistance.

If you leave those wandering thoughts unchecked, however, you're headed for a ditch. You could get to the point where you are so riddled with insecurity that you don't even know who you are anymore, so you're looking around for other people to emulate and finding that you don't measure up against them. That's because you're not supposed to measure up against them. That's like trying to measure how many gallons are in a mile. It's two totally different units of measurement because you are two totally different people.

I once heard a story about Dolly Parton entering a Dolly Parton look-alike contest. And guess what? She lost.[1] The people who were judging her, couldn't even recognize the real thing when it was staring them in the face. We all have a tendency to think that others are better at "our thing" than we are. Maybe we've even had other people tell us that. But God isn't holding a look-alike contest. He knows that there is only one you. He created you to be a unique individual with unique things to offer the world.

---

1. Anecdote from Dolly Parton's early life, widely reported in interviews and biographies.

Your job isn't to be the best at imitating someone who is already successful. Your job is to find out who your Father says you are.

I'm sure you've heard the Theodore Roosevelt quote that says, "Comparison is the thief of joy."[2] I'd like to take that a step further. Comparison doesn't just rob you of your joy, it robs you of your identity. It robs you of using everything that God put inside you to share with the world. It robs you of your individuality and turns you into a clone of who the world thinks you should be, and a cheap imitation at that.

Insecurity vs Security

If I asked you to tell me the opposite of insecurity, I'm sure you would probably say confidence, right? What I've learned is that the opposite of insecurity is actually security. Most of us have been led to believe that confidence is the ability to look like we've got it all together, and if we don't, you just have to "fake it 'til you make it."

But that's not what true confidence looks like. True confidence that comes from God is being *secure* in who He created you to be. There is no pretending. There is no striving. It's just acknowledgement. You are allowed to acknowledge the areas you're gifted in, while also acknowledging the areas where you fall short. That is what security looks like.

---

2. Commonly attributed to Theodore Roosevelt, though there is no documented source confirming this.

This is another area where I flat out believed the sneaky lies of the enemy. I would try to fight against my insecurities by pretending to be confident. I would walk into rooms with my head held high, making eye contact with anyone who would look at me, fighting the urge to tug at my clothes in the areas where they felt too tight. The thing is, that never felt authentic. That kind of confidence felt like a mask that didn't quite fit right. I was still crawling with insecurity. I still had a constant barrage of thoughts telling me what an imposter I was. The only difference was that now nobody could tell I was struggling, which also meant that no one could help me.

As soon as I made the shift into believing that it's okay for me to not be good at everything, I started relaxing a bit. Instead of obsessing over how I presented myself in the clothes I wore or the way I did my hair, I admitted to myself that I like to be more comfortable than put together and that's okay. Instead of forcing myself to be the type of person who carries themselves gracefully and always says and does the right thing, I simply started to acknowledge that I'm a little clumsy in more ways than one, but it's just a part of my charm. And do you know what I noticed? Some people still criticized me in all of the ways that I had feared. But other people loved me even more than they had before. Now I wasn't just being loved for who I pretended to be, I was being loved for who I was, at my very core.

Bring it to the Light

My all time favorite Disney movie is Beauty and the Beast. I used to watch that VHS on repeat. (For those of you who don't know, a VHS tape is how we dinosaurs used to watch movies back in the 1900s). There was something so comforting about that movie to me. It was all about a girl who felt ostracized from society all because she liked to mind her own business and read a lot of books. Honestly, same.

There was one scene in that movie in particular that always stuck with me. Belle is pleading with the Beast to let her father go and take her as prisoner instead. At that point, she asks the Beast to step into the light so she can see him clearly for the first time. He hesitantly inches his way forward until the light illuminates all of his grotesque features. And Belle reacts the same way we think most people will respond to our flaws. She gasps in horror and turns her face away.

There's a reason why we hide the things we struggle with. We are so afraid that if people knew our insecurities, it would cause people to recoil–that our vulnerability would punish us and leave us more broken than before. We think that nobody could possibly love those broken parts of us, so it's safer to tuck them out of sight so that nobody can reject us. But that's not the way Jesus responds.

Recently, a friend of mine and I were doing Bible study together when we had a revelation about this very thing. In Mark 3, we see Jesus healing a man with a withered hand. I want you to look closely at this so that I can point a few things out to you. First, check out verse 3. "Jesus said to the man with the shriveled hand, 'Stand up in front of everyone.'" Jesus wasn't trying to heal this man discreetly. He didn't schedule an appointment for later or lead him into some corner alley. He had him stand in front of the entire crowd, with his deepest insecurity on full display. Watch what he does next in verse 5, "He looked around at them in anger and, deeply distressed at their stubborn hearts, said to the man, 'Stretch out your hand.' He stretched it out, and his hand was completely restored."

Here's the kicker: Jesus didn't tell him which hand to stretch out. This man had a choice to make. He could either stretch out his good hand in hopes to impress the people and hide his struggles away for another day, *or* he could bring his deepest insecurities into the light. As we can see, he made the right choice. He stretched out his *withered* hand and it was completely restored, as if nothing had ever been wrong with it.

James 5:16 says, "Therefore confess your sins to each other and pray for each other so that you may be healed. The prayer of a righteous person is powerful and effective." The original word used for "sins" in this verse is paráptōma.[3] One of the definitions used for this word is "a deviation from the truth." If you are walking in insecurity, you have deviated from the truth of your identity. We have to be willing to confess these things to each other

---

3. Strong's Concordance: Strong's G3900 – παράπτωμα (paráptōma)

so that we can be healed from them. The easiest way to be set free from the bondage of your insecurity is to bring it to the light. Healing is waiting for you on the other side of your vulnerability. Confess it to someone you trust who can actually speak life into the situation and tell you the truth. Or, you can always bring it straight to Jesus. I hear that he's pretty good with that kind of thing.

Victory over Insecurity

The truth is, we all deal with insecurity from time to time, no matter how mature or experienced we are. There is no point in your life where you will arrive at a place where these struggles don't exist. At least, not until you get to heaven. Just because those mean little whispers come sneaking back in every now and then doesn't mean you've done anything wrong, and it doesn't mean that you're going backwards. It's just another opportunity to decide what you want to think about yourself.

I'll never forget hearing Brene Brown speak about the subject of insecurity and perfectionism.[4] What she said stopped me in my tracks and changed the way I saw my own struggle. She basically said that when we operate from a place of insecurity and strive for perfection, it keeps us from contributing to the world. We are so afraid of getting it wrong, of falling short, or opening ourselves

---

4. Brené Brown, in a YouTube interview on insecurity and perfectionism.

up to risk that we don't even try. Then she said, "At the end of my life, I want to be able to look back and say that I contributed more than I criticized." That led me to think about all of the times that I had neglected to contribute anything to the world around me because I was too busy criticizing myself. I was so hyper focused on making sure that I either showed up perfectly or not at all. And all it did was steal my creativity.

I tell my kids all the time that mistakes are okay because they help us grow. The only time mistakes hinder us is when we don't take the time to learn from them. So let me encourage you today. You don't have to hide all of your mistakes or your flaws. You are allowed to show up as you are, insecurities and all. You don't have to allow them to push you around anymore. Bring those things to the light. Let them be seen. Don't deviate from the truth of who God made you to be. And if you can do that, I think you'll find a freedom that you've never known before.

Chapter Six

Pride

When I was growing up back in the 90's, there used to be this cartoon that came on the Cartoon Network called "Johnny Bravo." To be honest, I can't even remember the plot of the show or what any of the episodes were about. All I remember is that Johnny Bravo was so self-absorbed it made me sick, even as a child. He was legitimately portrayed as someone who thought they were God's gift to earth. He was so obsessed with himself that he had no concept of what was happening with those around him. As humorous as this exaggerated portrayal was, I think we've all met someone at some point in our lives that falls into that category. That's the caricature that comes to mind when we think about the word "pride." We tend to think that pride is easily recognizable, so many of us make the mistake of thinking that it's a trap we won't fall into. But just like any other scheme of the enemy, pride is a slippery slope that nearly all of us have dealt with at some point or another.

You see, I've never really struggled with pride in the traditional sense of the word. I was never inclined to think about myself like Johnny Bravo does. I never thought I was God's gift to earth and never wanted to elevate myself above others. In fact, I almost always had the opposite problem. I had a tendency to think that I was a piece of garbage that had to fight my way into earning a seat at the table. If you had put me in a line-up with prisoners, liars, thieves and murderers and asked me who the worst person in the line-up was, I still probably would've pointed at myself. At that point in my life, I genuinely thought I had no value, because I wasn't aware of what I had to offer the world.

Then one day, I was listening to a podcast. I can't even remember what the podcast was called or who was talking, all I remember is that what they said changed my perspective forever. The main speaker said, "There are a lot of people who struggle with feeling worthless. They struggle with feeling like they matter less than everyone else." My ears perked up. *Ooh, he's talking about me,* I thought. He followed it up by saying, "That's called false humility. And it's a form of pride." *Excuse me?!* I nearly shouted at the radio. Until that whole point, I had lived my entire life thinking of others before I thought about myself, even to my own detriment. And yet here he was, basically telling me that I was being prideful. Who does this clown think he is? But then he continued, "You may convince yourself that you're thinking about others all of the time, but what you're really doing is measuring *yourself* against other people and feeling like you don't measure up. But you're still making it all about *you*." Well, at that point, he was just reading my mail. There was no denying the truth. I had fallen into the trap of false humility, thinking that was the only way to combat becoming arrogant. But just because you're running the opposite direction of something you know is wrong, doesn't mean you're on the right path. The truth usually lies somewhere in the middle, and from that point on, that was the path I set out to follow.

True Humility vs False Humility

True humility is defined as having an accurate assessment of one's worth.[1] I love that definition. You're not thinking too much of yourself or too little of yourself, you're just thinking about yourself a lot less. I remember coming to this crossroads when God told me that I needed to start thinking of myself as royalty (because I'm a daughter of the King) rather than a dirty sinner. It was a struggle for me to come into agreement with this new identity. But in order to have true humility, you have to be willing to acknowledge who you truly are.

I'll give you an example. The day I launched my first book[2] was one of the hardest mental battles I have ever faced. You would think that would be the easy part, right? I had just spent nearly half a year writing, editing, rewriting, re-editing, designing and

---

1. American Psychological Association, "What Is Humility?", 2018.

2. *7 Days to a Life of Limitless*

formatting this book. Launch day should have been cause for celebration. I was finally a published author. I had accomplished a lifelong dream that I never thought would even be possible. And yet there I was, standing in my kitchen, crying in my husband's arms about how much I felt like a failure. Why was that such a hard battle? Because false humility was nipping at my heels, telling me that no one would want to read the words that I had written. That everyone already knew the information I had to give. I felt like I had nothing of value to offer the world. I felt worthless. And yet, God had already written success into my story. He had already decided that the book was going to be successful; He just wanted me to write it.

Over the course of the next year, that book (7 Days to a Life of Limitless) sold about 10,000 copies. Not because of my own skill and ability, but because I simply said yes to what God was asking me to do. I say this not to brag on myself, but to brag on God. If I had gotten out of my own way and come into agreement with what God was doing in my life, I could've spared myself a lot of pain and heartache along the way. If I had been walking in true humility that day, my attitude would've been totally different. I would have been able to acknowledge that the success or downfall of the book had very little to do with me and everything to do with God. I would've recognized that Him asking me to write the book was just an invitation to step into what He was already doing, and it wasn't dependent on me to carry the weight of that assignment. I just got to be a part of it.

When you operate in true humility, it's kind of like floating down a river. The current is what carries you. How much effort you add to it is of little consequence in the long run. Here's the thing, friend. God's not asking you to carry it all yourself, He's just asking you to step into the water and float. Don't focus on your own ability, on whether you're succeeding or failing. Just say yes to whatever He wants to do in your life.

Here's the tricky part about humility, though. When you start to step into your God-given identity and embrace true humility, there will still be people who accuse you of being prideful. Anytime you start to assume your rightful place, natural elevation will come. It's the way God works. Does that mean you'll have everything you ever wanted and your life will be super easy? No. In fact, it's sometimes quite the opposite. It just means that people will start to take notice of what God is doing in you and through you. Because when it's truly God, His works don't go unnoticed by everyone. And because of that natural influence, you may have people accuse you of trying to make a name for yourself.

I don't say this to scare you, but to prepare you. It's normal. And not enough people talk about it. We see all of these great leaders of the faith. Preachers, prophets, missionaries. We notice their amazing works and seem to naturally believe that their lives are incredible. That they don't struggle. That no one ever has anything bad to say about them. But of course they do. You don't get to any level of influence without a nearly equal level of opposition. But when that time does come, you can take heart that you are not alone. David's brothers said the same thing about him. So did

Joseph's. I can't even tell you the amount of people who attacked me when my book started gaining traction. I was accused of everything from "profiting off of God" to leading others astray. When you walk in true humility, it will look prideful to anyone who is still trapped in anything else. But hear me when I say this. It's not your job to convince them. You don't have anything to prove. People don't need you to explain that you're just following God the best you can. The right people will see it and take notice. And they will love you for it. Because the fruit that you're producing is feeding *them* and that's all that matters.

Fruit Comes Naturally

Can I just take this a little further? Because I really want to say something that I believe is going to set you free right now. The end result is not up to you. I know that's all you've been told. Even in the Christian culture, we've been fed this idea that we have to produce, produce, produce if we want to be useful. But have you ever seen a fruit tree straining to produce fruit? I don't know about you but I've never heard my pear tree grunting during the spring as those first pears start to appear. That's because there is no striving involved. The fruit is naturally produced because of what the tree is being *fed*. And here's another thing: the tree isn't feeding itself either. That tree sits there and trusts that everything it needs will be provided for it. And because of the overflow of energy and nutrients, fruit naturally comes forth.

Pride tries to tell you that everything is dependent on *your* behavior, *your* input, *your* performance. The people who do well are tempted to become prideful, the ones who struggle to measure up typically succumb to false humility. Either way, it's all about what you can do, not about who you are. No wonder you've been struggling so much with your self worth. You've been carrying something that was never meant to be put on your shoulders in the first place. Because even though you do have a part to play, you were never meant to be in charge of the outcome.

Remember when God told Moses to go to Pharaoh and ask to let His people go? The whole story can be found in Exodus 3. Moses tried every trick in the book to weasel his way out of that assignment. Why? Because he was dependent on what *he* could do. He was focused on *his* speech impediment, *his* background, *his* inability. No wonder the Bible says God got angry at him. I would have too. Because God was just trying to invite Moses to be a part of what he already wanted to do. But Moses was more focused on himself than he was on God.

When we step into true humility, what we're really doing is removing the weight from our own shoulders and placing it in God's hands. This comes from realizing that it's not about what we can do, it's about what God can do through us. In Matthew 11:28-30, Jesus says, "Come to me, all you who are weary and burdened, and I will give you rest. Take my yoke upon you and learn from me, for I am gentle and humble in heart, and you will find rest for your souls. For my yoke is easy and my burden is light."

Joshua and Caleb had a solid understanding of this concept when the Israelites were in the wilderness (Numbers 13).Wh ile everyone else was saying that it was impossible to take the Promised Land (because they were depending on their own ability), Joshua and Caleb were confident that Israel could take the land because they knew they only had to depend on God's ability. They weren't trying to figure out how to make it work. They weren't crunching numbers or creating strategies. They just rested in the knowledge of who God is and who they were to him.

Listen to me, friend. You may think that if you push harder, try more, and be better that God will somehow be more pleased with you. All He's ever asked you to do is approach him, despite all of the opposition that may be in the way. Matthew 6:33 says, "But seek first his kingdom and his righteousness, and all these things will be given to you as well." It doesn't say that if you seek his kingdom first then he will show you how to earn everything else. It says they will be added to you. Given to you. Placed into your lap. No striving required. It's not on you, friend. Just get yourself out of the way so God can do what he does best.

You're Not a Lone Wolf

My daughter is currently three years old. One of her favorite things to say is, "I can do it all by myself. I'm a big girl." She's learning how to be independent, but sometimes, there really are things she wants to handle on her own that she really shouldn't. Painting her own fingernails, for example. Thank goodness she uses the water-based polish that wipes right off of all of the surfaces she manages to get it on. As cute as it is when we're children, sometimes we have a tendency to carry these same beliefs into adulthood. When problems arise, we think we should be able to handle it ourselves for one reason or another. Maybe it's because we don't want other people to perceive us as weak. Or it could be that we are so convinced that our problems are burdens that we don't want to inconvenience those we love the most. No matter how you slice it, that's pride talking.

Pride may feel like protection, but it's really a form of isolation. It keeps you from discovering who will actually show up for you when times get difficult because your pride won't let anyone close enough to try. It locks out the love that you crave so badly and then convinces you that it's safer that way. Can I just tell you something? You were never meant to be a lone wolf. In fact, no one is.

No, really, lone wolves are a made up thing, even in nature.[3] Wolves travel in packs and when they find a partner, they mate for life. Yes, occasionally a wolf will voluntarily leave their pack or be pushed out of it, but they never remain alone. When they leave one pack, they set out to find another. There's no such thing as a lone wolf. At least, not for long. It's not the way God created us. We were made for family. That's why the Bible says, "Two are better than one, because they have a good return for their labor:

---

3. L. David Mech, Wolves: Behavior, Ecology, and Conservation (Chicago: University of Chicago Press, 2003).

If either of them falls down, one can help the other up. But pity anyone who falls and has no one to help them up." (Ecclesiastes 4:9-10). Long-term isolation goes against the very nature that God gave us.

If you are lucky enough to have found yourself in a group of people who love and support you, pride can try to sabotage those relationships too. It may convince you to compare yourself to others, or to convince you that you could do a better job than someone else is doing. What we have to remember is that we're all designed to compliment each other. My strengths may compliment another person's weaknesses and vice versa. We each play a significant part in the body of Christ. Honestly, nobody explains this better than Paul does. I want you to take a look at this whole passage because it's just too good to chop up. This comes from 1 Corinthians 12-27.

> "Just as a body, though one, has many parts, but all its many parts form one body, so it is with Christ. For we were all baptized by one Spirit so as to form one body—whether Jews or Gentiles, slave or free—and we were all given the one Spirit to drink. Even so the body is not made up of one part but of many. Now if the foot should say, 'Because I am not a hand, I do not belong to the body,' it would not for that reason stop being part of the body. And if the ear should say, 'Because I am not an eye, I do not belong to the body,' it would not for that reason

> stop being part of the body. If the whole body were an eye, where would the sense of hearing be? If the whole body were an ear, where would the sense of smell be? But in fact God has placed the parts in the body, every one of them, just as he wanted them to be. If they were all one part, where would the body be? As it is, there are many parts, but one body. The eye cannot say to the hand, 'I don't need you!' And the head cannot say to the feet, 'I don't need you!' On the contrary, those parts of the body that seem to be weaker are indispensable, and the parts that we think are less honorable we treat with special honor. And the parts that are unpresentable are treated with special modesty, while our presentable parts need no special treatment. But God has put the body together, giving greater honor to the parts that lacked it, so that there should be no division in the body, but that its parts should have equal concern for each other. If one part suffers, every part suffers with it; if one part is honored, every part rejoices with it. Now you are the body of Christ, and each one of you is a part of it."

When we begin to think of ourselves not as a lone wolf, or a burden, but a part of a larger body of people, that's when we remember that we are all a kingdom family. There is no room for comparison in the family of God. When I win, you win. When you win, I win. When any of us wins, God wins. And isn't that all that really matters?

I remember when my husband, Josh, and I were dating, a local grocery store was having a giveaway for a set of patio furniture. So we each wrote down our names and phone numbers and dropped them into the box. Later that day, we were hanging out at Josh's house when he got a phone call. His name had been drawn as the winner of the giveaway. His mom, overhearing the conversation, excitedly exclaimed, "We won a new patio table!" Her name wasn't drawn, but because she and Josh were in the same family, she knew that a win for him was a win for her. And the whole family got to enjoy the benefits of that patio table for years.

Don't let pride convince you that you're better off on your own. Don't rob yourself of the benefits of belonging to a kingdom family. Ask for help when you need it. Acknowledge that other people are willing and able to support you. Because the moment you lay your pride aside is the moment you make room for belonging.

Victory Over Pride

Whether you're a Johnny Bravo or a Debbie Downer, my guess is that pride has slipped into your life in some way, shape or form. Pride is something that doesn't discriminate. It either convinces you that you are too much or not enough. And it is a disease that has contaminated every single person on the planet. But just like any other disease, it's something you must heal from. We try to convince ourselves that eventually, these struggles will just work themselves out. "Time heals all wounds," we say, as if we just have to wait it out. Well, I want to challenge that idea. Because even though time may heal some wounds, it can also infect the wounds we leave untreated.

There's a reason you picked up this book. And my best guess is because you're feeling defeated and you're tired of it. Nobody picks up a book called *Leaving Defeat* if everything is going well in their life. In order to heal whatever wounds have been keeping you stuck in that place of defeat, your pride is going to have to die. And you're going to have to be the one to kill it.

I get it. That's *hard.* It is not easy to look someone in the eyes and tell them that you are desperate for help, knowing that you are opening yourself up to the risk of being brushed off. It's not easy to finally make that phone call to set up an appointment for counseling, knowing you will have to face down those demons when you get there. It's not easy to even admit that this struggle might be a little too complicated for you to handle on your own. But it has to be done.

Here's the deal. You deserve to heal. You are worth it. Jesus sure seemed to think so when he came to die on the cross for you. You didn't think he died just for your salvation, did you? I mean, that is part of it, but he also died so that you could experience what it's like to live an eternal life free from all of this torment. Free from the pain, the struggle, the hardship. He wants you to experience a taste of that freedom here, "on earth as it is in heaven." (Matthew 6:10). But in order to do that, you're going to have to heal. And in order to heal, you've got to kill your pride. It won't be easy. Things that bring us great satisfaction rarely are. But what I can promise you is that when you step into that level of humility, your eyes will be opened to everything your pride has blinded you to. You'll be able to see and experience the world with fresh eyes. And you will discover more fulfillment than you ever thought possible.

Chapter Seven

People Pleasing

Most of us would probably say that one of the deepest desires is to be known and loved for who we truly are. Wouldn't you agree? So it makes sense that we are desperate for the validation of others. We can't stand the thought of someone thinking that we are selfish or arrogant or cowardly. So, at times, we all do things that are a little bit outside of our true nature in order to gain the affection or attention of those around us. It's like a little white lie that we tell, but that little white lie comes with the shiny reward of other people's approval. No wonder we keep doing it.

People pleasing can seem like a very natural and harmless way to keep the peace with others, but I want to make you aware of the real dangers of it. There's an old Native American folk tale called "The Wolf and the Blade."[1] In this story, a hunter is trying

1. Ruth S. Newton, *Folk Tales of American Indians*, Dover Publications, 2002.

to kill the wolf without any direct confrontation with it. What the hunter does is coat the blade of his knife in ice and then soak the ice in blood. He then sticks the knife, blade up, into the ground and waits for the wolf to smell the blood and come looking for it. The wolf finally approaches and begins licking the blade. At first, it satisfies his craving without having any adverse effects. But over time, the ice begins to thaw and the blade of the knife is exposed. Now, the blood that the wolf is tasting is his own, but he can't tell the difference. If he doesn't become aware of this self-destructive behavior soon, the wolf will bleed to death without ever knowing what hit him.

Whenever we lean into people pleasing, whether we know it or not, we are caught in the same trap as the wolf, shedding our own blood and not even realizing it. At first, it seems harmless, but eventually, it is to our own detriment. Because eventually, you get to a point where you don't even know who you are anymore without taking cues from someone else on how you should behave or who you should be. In all actuality, people pleasing is just an inconsistency in our character. It leaves us constantly shifting around, blending in like a chameleon, morphing and contorting to fit the mold. And at that point, nobody knows who you are. Not even you.

One of the most notorious examples of people pleasing comes from the story of Jesus' own crucifixion. Before Jesus is sentenced to death, he is arrested and handed over to Pilate. (Matthew 27). Here's where the situation gets sticky. Pilate can't find a good reason to sentence him. He *knows* that Jesus is innocent. But because of the uproar of the people, he sentences God's own Son to death and releases a hardened criminal instead. All because he didn't want to deal with the aftermath of the angry crowd.

Of course, we know that things had to happen this way. Jesus had to die as an innocent man or we would not be freed from our sins. Even still, I can't help but wonder what Pilate must've felt like after the fact. He had tried to wash his hands clean of Jesus' blood, but my guess is that he did that because he already knew it was wrong and chose to give in anyway. Listen, you can try and convince yourself all you want that when it comes to the really big stuff, you will take a stand when it actually matters. But if you can't take a stand for what's right even in the smallest of instances, what makes you think you'll actually be able to do that when it really counts?

I remember getting to this point in my own life. Little by little, I let other people's opinions shape me into who I thought they wanted me to be. Over time these little decisions to hide who I really was and stifle my own opinions led me to a point where I had lost all sense of self. I truly did not know who I was anymore. My husband would tell me that he loved me and I would say, "Why? Everything I have to offer you could be replaced tomorrow with someone else." He would usually respond by saying something like, "I don't love you for what you do for me, I love you for who you are." But that just confused me even further. How can he love me for who I am when I don't even know who I am?

Thankfully, Jesus tells us exactly who we are. We no longer have to guess. We no longer have to learn how to read people so that we can adapt to their moods or their standards. All it takes is a little courage to be consistent in our character, even if that means it won't be popular with everyone.

Salt is Abrasive, Light is Blinding

Have you ever been driving down the road at night and seen an approaching vehicle that has those fancy LED headlights? Even when they are set to the dimmest setting, it's still enough to blind anyone for a solid 30 seconds after the car has already passed. It can be really annoying, can't it? That's because light is offensive to those who are adjusted to the darkness.

In Matthew 5:14-16, Jesus says, "You are the light of the world. A town built on a hill cannot be hidden. Neither do people light a lamp and put it under a bowl. Instead they put it on its stand, and it gives light to everyone in the house. In the same way, let your light shine before others, that they may see your good deeds and glorify your Father in heaven." I know most of us learned the song in Sunday school about "This Little Light of Mine," but let me tell you something. There is nothing little about your light. I don't know who lied to you, but you are not meant to be some sweet little candle tucked quietly away in a corner somewhere. You are meant to illuminate the whole area until darkness can no longer show its face when you're around. And that kind of light? It's offensive. It's irritating. It's annoying to people whose eyes are well-adjusted to the dark. But that doesn't mean that you're meant to hide it for the sake of their comfort.

If we go back to Matthew 5 and back up to verse 13, this is what it says, "You are the salt of the earth. But if the salt loses its saltiness, how can it be made salty again? It is no longer good for anything, except to be thrown out and trampled underfoot." Do you want to know something interesting about salt? It's an agitator.

Did you know that in a survival scenario, salt can be used as one of the methods for purifying water? In this case, if you came across some water that was impure, you could add some salt to it to filter out some of the suspended particles in a process called flocculation.[2] Basically what happens is the salt agitates the impurities in the water, disrupting their ability to integrate themselves. The particles then start to bond together and become heavy, causing them to settle at the bottom of the container. From there, they can be more easily filtered out, leaving behind purer, cleaner, safer drinking water.

We even see this message being demonstrated in 2 Kings 2. Let's look at the story that takes place in verses 19-22.

> The people of the city said to Elisha, "Look, our lord, this town is well situated, as you can see, but the water is bad and the land is unproductive." "Bring me a new bowl," he said, "and put salt in it." So they brought it to him. Then he went out to the spring and threw the salt into it, saying, "This is

---

2. Australian Safety and Compensation Council, Water Purification Methods for Survival, 2010.

> what the Lord says: 'I have healed this water. Never again will it cause death or make the land unprod uctive.'" And the water has remained pure to this day, according to the word Elisha had spoken.

Now, I'm not saying that the little bit of salt Elisha sprinkled into the water was able to filter out all of the impurities in that spring. Obviously, that story was demonstrating a Divine miracle, but the message behind the miracle remains the same. Salt is meant to purify things. It's meant to draw out impurities. It's meant to preserve and sustain things. So if you are the salt of the earth, don't you think that means you'll be a little agitating to the impurities in the people around you?

I understand that this is not a fun identity statement to lean into. Nobody *wants* to be an agitator. Nobody *wants* to be annoying. Well, maybe some people get a kick out of it (ahem...older brothers), but I think the majority of us could say that that's not our goal. But if you are actively living out your role as the salt and light of the earth, it's bound to happen at some point. When people get irritated with you, it's not necessarily because you're doing anything wrong. In fact, it could be an indicator that you're doing it right.

One thing that I learned from my husband very early on in our relationship is that you should never say something behind someone's back that you wouldn't be willing to say to their face. It doesn't matter if he likes you or not, if my husband hears someone talking bad about you behind your back, he will shut it down.

It's one of the things I admire most about him. And it's a solid motto to live by, because it honors the people around you, and allows you to speak without worrying that what you say will get back to someone. Honestly, that's the example we see Jesus setting too. He wasn't afraid to speak the truth, but he always did it with the intention of loving people well. You never see an example of Jesus back-biting or gossiping. And if he did say something that wouldn't be super fun to hear, he made sure to say it right to the person's face.

A little while ago, I bumped into a situation that put my salt and light role to the test. I was in a room where someone was very frustrated with another person. In their frustration, they were saying things about this person that I'm sure they didn't mean. Let's be honest, we've all been there, right? But even though I understood that kind of frustration, I was still grieved by the fact that there seemed to be no grace. I thought about how God might view the situation as a parent. If I overheard one of my kids saying those same words about my other child, my heart would shatter into a million pieces. So, in the moment, I decided to try and redirect this person's anger by saying, "I'm sure the person you're frustrated with is just doing the best that they can."

I wish I could say that my well-intentioned correction was met with love and understanding. I wish I could tell you that the person saw the heart behind my words. They did not. In fact, it led to some pretty damaging consequences that took a while to patch up. But if you were to ask me if I regret my choices that day, I would have to say no. After being met with such an aftershock, it really led me to examine my words, choices, and intentions carefully and prayerfully. And I can honestly say that after asking God to take a close look at my own heart, He assured me that I was doing the best I could to honor my Father, and I don't regret that. Could I have said it in a different way that might have been better received? Maybe. But we can split hairs all day long.

The truth of the matter is that if someone is not in the right headspace, they're not going to receive corrections well no matter how you put it. Does that mean you should just let the moment pass you by for the sake of not rocking the boat? I think that would depend on the Holy Spirit's guidance at that moment. But if you're measuring God's approval by how well people respond to you, you're using the wrong standard.

I used to do the same thing. I thought if people didn't react well to what I said, I must be saying it wrong. Until God reminded me of the story of Moses. Moses was complaining to God about this very same thing. He was essentially saying, "God, I can't do this. Nothing I say comes out right." Remember God's response? Here's what He says in Exodus 4:11-12. "The Lord said to him, 'Who gives man his mouth? Who makes him deaf or dumb? Who gives him sight or makes him blind? It is I, the Lord. Now, go! I will help you to speak, and I will tell you what to say.'"

God Himself was going to give Moses the exact words to say to Pharaoh. And when he did speak these words, what was Pharaoh's response? Anger. We cannot look to people to indicate how well we are doing in our attempts to please God. People will not always respond well, and that's okay. We just have to make sure that when they do react in anger, we still love them well.

I was recently having a conversation with someone who was struggling with the idea of loving your neighbor as yourself. This person said to me, "I just find them very difficult to love. There is literally nothing appealing about this person's attitude. I just don't like them very much." To which I replied, "I don't think anyone likes the unhealed version of anyone." We have to remember that when we are dealing with people who are extremely difficult to love, it's often because they are extremely wounded. When we get to heaven, everyone will be healed and whole and we will all get along just fine. There will be no gossiping in heaven. No drama. No one will call you a mean name or hurl a hurtful insult your way ever again. But down here, we have to deal with trauma, heartache, outbursts, and more. So, no, we're not going to like everyone. But that doesn't mean they're an awful person, it just means they're not walking in their identity.

Ten years ago, you probably wouldn't have liked me either. I was afraid of my own shadow, deeply jaded, passive aggressive and immature. None of those things are appealing. But that wasn't me. That was the false identity that I had adopted because of the pain I had gone through. I wasn't walking in my identity. So when we're dealing with people, we have to look past their mistakes and their outbursts and try to see them the way that God does, with pure love and understanding.

As long as you are following God's guidance to the best of your ability and speaking from a place of love in your heart for the individual you're speaking to, you've done your part. The outcome is not up to you. Just like in the story I told you earlier, I followed the Spirit's lead to the best of my ability and it didn't go well. But rather than gaining favor with other people, I gained the confidence to stand on my own two feet despite opposition. I believe that was the lesson I was meant to learn all along.

Rejection

Listen, I get it. The reason why most of us are drawn to pleasing people is because we want to avoid the painful sting of rejection. When you open yourself up to someone and are vulnerable and honest, that vulnerability and honesty can sometimes be met with flat out dismissal. And that hurts just as much as any physical pain ever could. I think the mistake that we often make is thinking that rejection is an indicator of our value, as if the way people treat us determines our worth, but that's simply not true.

Let me tell you about the time I learned this lesson. Right around the time my husband and I got engaged, I finally felt like I was starting to blossom into adulthood. As a kid, I would watch shows like *Friends* and *How I Met Your Mother* and crave that kind of life. In my mind, those characters had it all. Sure, their lives weren't perfect, but they had the one thing I wanted more than anything in the world. They had people to share their life with. But not just any people. They had a tight-knit group of friends. A chosen family. And that family was what carried them through all of the tragedy and heartache in their lives. Their group was just full of people who didn't leave. As a kid who was mostly introverted and isolated, and who struggled with feeling that type of rejection everywhere I turned, that kind of life seemed like an absolute dream.

At one point, I thought I had found it. Josh and I had been grafted into a group of friends who just did life together. All of a sudden, I went from feeling chronically alone to having people who wanted us to come over for Thanksgiving and Christmas and everything in between. Any given weekend, we would all spend time together, whether we were riding four wheelers or hanging out at someone's house. It didn't really matter what we did, as long as we were together. I finally felt like I had a place in this world among people who chose me. That is, until the day it all came to a screeching halt.

For two years, we had spent nearly every weekend with these people. And then one day, we just stopped getting invited. None of our friends would answer our calls or texts. They wouldn't have a conversation with us and tell us what happened or what we had done to offend them. We weren't even given the opportunity to try and make it right.

Meanwhile, I had to see all of the pictures that they posted on Facebook, laughing and enjoying their time together as if I had never existed in their lives. I had never felt so disposable. No one tells you about the kind of grieving that comes with having to mourn the loss of people who are still alive but just stopped choosing you. No one teaches you how to deal with that kind of pain. And so, for a long time, I didn't know how to cope. It took me two years before I even wanted to open my heart back up to the potential of trying again.

I wish I could say that I never think about that time. That I'm completely healed and whole and it never even left a scar–but I can't. Friendships are something that hold such a soft spot for me because I have so much love in my heart and have such a deep desire to share that love with other people. And when people take the most valuable gift you have to offer and shred it right in front of you, it's not something you just get over.

Over time, however, I learned to look at the situation from a different perspective. The more time I was alone in the aftermath of that loss, the more time I spent with Jesus. And the more time I spent with Jesus, the more he taught me that my value is not something that's negotiable. And the same goes for you. Your value is not up for debate. You see, the whole time I was grieving the loss of these friendships, I had been looking at it as if their rejection *determined* my worth. Because they did not value the things I had to offer, I concluded that those things must not be valuable. Therefore, I have nothing to offer. And when you feel as though you have no value, you feel as though any hope for your future has withered away. No wonder we change everything about ourselves in order to be accepted. In a world where rejection runs rampant, the scariest thing we can ever be is ourselves.

Here's what I learned through my process of healing, and here's what I want you to know. Just because someone can't see your value doesn't mean you're not valuable. In Matthew 7:6, Jesus says, "Do not give dogs what is sacred; do not throw your pearls to pigs. If you do, they may trample them under their feet, and turn and tear you to pieces." If you had a $100 bill, would you ever give it to your dog and expect them to take care of it? Of course not. Dogs cannot even begin to comprehend the value of money. So why do we continue to give our most valuable gifts to the people who seem to appreciate them the least? I think it's because all of us are in search of belonging. But let me tell you something. Not everywhere you fit is where you belong. If you have to beg for a seat at the table, you don't belong at that table.

Our self worth should only ever come from one place. It should come from the one who determined our value before we ever took a breath. It should come from the one who decided we were valuable enough to die for before we were even born. 1 Peter 1:19 says, "You were bought with the precious blood of Christ's death. He was a pure and perfect sacrificial Lamb." Now, imagine yourself writing on a price tag the value of the life of God's one and only Son, who was flawless and blameless in every way. What do you think that price would be? Priceless, right? There is no number known to man that could put a value on God's love for us. So take that price tag and stick it on yourself. Because that's exactly the price he paid for you.

Jackson Pollock is an artist that is famously known for his paintings that look a lot like paint splattered on a canvas. One of the most expensive paintings he ever sold was a canvas no larger than four feet in length. It sold for $200 million.[3] Someone may look at that painting and decide that it looks like chicken scratch. They may argue that it's not even worth $5 because their two year old could paint something similar. But that person would never in a million years be able to go out and buy a Jackson Pollock painting for $5. Because they are not the one that determines its value. The creator of the painting is the only one who can determine its worth. And your Creator is the only one who can determine yours.

Do you see what I'm saying? It's not up to anyone else to say how much value you have because they are not the ones who are allowed to put a price on you. Jesus already paid for you and determined that your worth was absolutely priceless, and no one else, no matter how hard they try, can change that. Still, rejection can sting even if you know how valuable you are to your Father. We just have to remember that healthy, healed, whole people are not going to be the ones rejecting us. I'm sure you've heard the phrase "hurt people, hurt people." When we deal with rejection, what we're really dealing with is an unhealed wound in the person who hurt us.

It's a game-changer when you realize that other people's rejection of you says more about their wounds than your worth, but even with that clarity, we still have to be careful about who we

---

3. Jackson Pollock's Number 17A (1948) reportedly sold for $200 million, one of the highest prices ever paid for a painting.

choose to invest our time in. We cannot keep throwing ourselves into relationships with people that are not capable of protecting what's sacred. God values your heart. He's not asking you to pass it around like a party favor. We owe everyone love, but we don't owe everyone unfettered access to our hearts. You can love people well without investing everything you have into their lives. Save that treasure for the people who will cherish it.

Victory over People Pleasing

Every weekend, when my husband is off work, he will get up slightly earlier than me and head to the kitchen to start a pot of coffee. A few minutes later, he will walk into our bedroom with two coffee mugs in his hands. One black with a single scoop of sugar, one with two scoops of sugar and a healthy dose of caramel creamer. I'll let you guess which one is mine. We both enjoy drinking coffee together, but our coffee preferences are drastically different. That's because we're different people. God designed us that way. We each have unique likes and dislikes. There is no uniformity. Can you imagine how boring that would be if there were? Imagine if all coffee were the same and you couldn't get a mocha frappe one day and an oat milk latte the next. That sounds awful.

I don't know about you, but I love the variety. Being a highly creative person means that my moods and preferences change like the wind. Whenever people ask me what my favorite color is, I never know how to answer because it will probably be different next week. How is anyone supposed to pick a favorite of anything? There's too much beauty and variety in the world to zero in on just one thing.

Now, imagine trying to adapt to my ever-evolving, ever-changing preferences. Can you imagine how exhausting that would be? And yet, people who struggle with people pleasing are not only trying to adapt to just one person's changing inclinations, they're trying to adapt to every single solitary person around them. That's *a lot* of hard work. No wonder we're so exhausted. We're spending all of our energy running on a hamster wheel that has no end in sight.

While I have always struggled with people pleasing, my husband has not. He has remained constant throughout the entirety of our relationship. Sure, his moods can fluctuate a bit based on what's happening in his life at the moment, but who he is at his core always remains the same. At the end of the day, I know what to expect with him. I know what's going to bother him and what's not. I know that if I text him and tell him I'm bringing home a stray animal, he will act annoyed but will wind up falling in love with it too. I know that if someone is gossiping about someone else in front of him, he will shut it down. I know that if there's a need to be met, he will do everything in his power to meet it. And the reason I know all of these things is because those are character traits of his that do not change. They remain constant. Secure. They are the pieces of his personality that do not shift based on who happens to be around him at any given moment.

Honestly, he may not be everyone's cup of coffee. But he is mine. All of those qualities are the things that I appreciate most about him. I can't help but think of how sad it would be if he quit letting me bring stray animals home because he was worried someone would think he was a pushover. Or if he stopped standing up for what's right because he was worried about offending someone. Or if he resisted the urge to be generous because he was concerned about people accusing him of showing off. It would devastate me if he chose to hide those parts of himself and only bring them out when the right people were looking. Yet, I'm so guilty of doing just that.

One night, I was praying about this very thing. I was telling God how afraid I was to show certain parts of myself. I was confiding in Him about how afraid I was to open myself up to that rejection. He responded with a vision. Honestly, are you surprised? In this vision, I was standing in a room by myself. In this room was a single table and two chairs. On the table was a puzzle that formed a picture of me. I could hear someone coming, so I quickly started picking out all of the puzzle pieces that I thought were ugly or undesirable. As I scrambled to pick out these pieces, the door swung open and a friend of mine walked in. Startled, I dropped all of the pieces in my hands. As they fell to the floor, I quickly bent down to scoop them all up and try to hide them. My friend knelt down and picked one up. "Are these pieces of you?" they asked, "Why are you trying to hide them?" "Because they're ugly," I replied. My friend sat in one of the chairs and patted the other one, motioning for me to sit too. "That may be true," they said, "but they're part of you. Come on. Bring all of you to the table." We finished putting the picture back together. Once we were done, they said, "There. That's all of you. And that's a beautiful picture."

Gosh, every time I think about that vision, I get a little teary-eyed. Because it perfectly illustrates the way God sees us. He's proud of what he made when he made you, even with all of the flaws and broken pieces that developed along the way. It kind of reminds me of my favorite t-shirt. I've had it for years. The neck is stretched out, and it is threadbare and full of holes. But every time my husband threatens to throw it out, I tell him he can pry it out of my cold dead hands. I don't care about the imperfections it has sustained along the way. I keep it because it's my favorite. And I'm pretty sure you're far more valuable to God than my favorite t-shirt is to me. We get so fixated on trying to be perfect, do everything right, and not rock the boat that we forget we are not meant to throw out all the broken pieces, but to bring them all to the table so that God can use them to create a beautiful picture.

Yes, you're going to experience rejection and ridicule when you shed light on the parts of you that feel the most vulnerable, because you're not everyone's cup of coffee. But when you remove those parts of yourself, you're also robbing yourself of the love that you will experience from those people that love and appreciate everything you have to offer, flaws and all.

Chapter Eight

Victimhood

Take a deep breath for me. In fact, why don't you go ahead and take another one. And then buckle up your metaphorical seatbelt because this subject is a doozy. It's one that's all too familiar to me. I used to set up my mental workshop in victimhood. It was my residential address for a season of my life. I know better than anyone what it's like to feel like life is happening to you and there's nothing you can do about it. Thankfully, that also means I know how to talk you through it.

The thing about the victimhood mindset is that it's a total shapeshifter. It can show up in many ways and sometimes can be tricky to spot. Maybe sometimes it shows up as self-deprecating humor because you genuinely think that you're a piece of garbage. The Bible does say, "Out of the heart the mouth speaks," after all. (Matthew 12:34). Most of the time it looks like wallowing in our pain and self-pity. That was my preferred method of torture for many years. But then other times, it can simply look like apathy. Maybe we just think that our actions are of little consequence because we think that *we* are of little consequence. Whichever way you spin it, the victimhood mindset is all about feeling helpless.

About a decade ago, after a particularly traumatic string of events, my victimhood mindset hit an all time low. I spiraled into the deepest darkest depression that I had ever known. I didn't even know it was possible to feel so low and still be breathing. All I seemed to be able to manage was laying in my bed all day. My family had no idea how to help me because nothing they said seemed to make a difference. I was drowning, and nobody seemed to have a life raft. It wasn't that I necessarily wanted to die, but I prayed every night that God wouldn't wake me up in the morning because the pain felt too great to endure. I genuinely felt as if there was no hope left. As if there was nothing more that I could do to drag myself out of this pit. One thing you have to understand about depression is that it feels like a prison that you are incapable of escaping. So when someone is stuck in that cell for too long, it's normal to wonder if they will ever make it out.

I kept wondering *Why did God let those things happen to me, knowing that I couldn't stop them? Why isn't He rescuing me from this?* And yet, day after day, I would wake up in the morning trying to find the will to get out of bed and get dressed, and I would have the same recurring vision of Jesus sitting on the bed beside me, holding my hand, not saying a word. For some reason, I always thought that he would try to encourage me, or tell me to get up, or give me a reason to keep fighting. But he never did. He just sat there, unspeaking. It was almost as if he was trying to say, "I'm here. I'm not leaving you. And I don't care how long it takes."

That situation reminded me of Psalm 34:18, "The Lord is close to the brokenhearted and saves those who are crushed in spirit."

During that time in my life, Jesus never rushed my pain, and I'm not here to rush yours. But, over time, He began to slowly unveil things to me that changed my perspective on suffering and pain, which allowed me to come out the other side victorious. Those are the lessons I want to share with you. Listen, friend, I'm not here to tell you to snap out of it. I'm not here to give you a list of reasons why you're being ridiculous. I don't think you're being ridiculous at all, I think you're being a *human.* And although the grief feels heavy right now, I want you to know that there is always light at the end of this tunnel. If you can't see it yet, allow me to point the way.

Suffering Serves a Purpose

I know a lot of people have the question, "If God is so loving, why does he allow his children to suffer in the first place?" Honestly, I've asked that same question. I've learned that sometimes it's important not to just shrug your shoulders and accept that you'll never know the answer. Some questions require wrestling. Just like in Genesis 32, when Jacob wrestled with God in the wilderness, refusing to let go until he was blessed, there are some questions that require the same amount of determination. In fact, there are several stories in the Bible about the power of persistence. Jacob's story was only one of them.

In Luke 18, Jesus tells a parable about a widow who persistently seeks justice from a corrupt judge. In the end, it was her relentless persistence that convinced the judge to rule in her favor. Then in Luke 11, we see another story about a man who persistently knocks on his friend's door at midnight asking for bread. After denying his request multiple times, his friend finally gives up and gives him bread. What I'm trying to get you to see here is that persistence pays off. God *wants* you to have the answers to your questions, some answers are just buried a little deeper than others. Let's look at Matthew 7:7-11 together. See if you can spot the Father's heart for you in these verses.

> "'Ask and it will be given to you; seek and you will find; knock and the door will be opened to you. For everyone who asks receives; the one who seeks finds; and to the one who knocks, the door will be opened. Which of you, if your son asks for bread, will give him a stone? Or if he asks for a fish, will give him a snake? If you, then, though you are evil, know how to give good gifts to your children, how much more will your Father in heaven give good gifts to those who ask him!'"

Do you see what I mean? God isn't some mean old man up in the sky waiting to punish you for all the ways you mess up. He's a good Father who never gets bothered by your questions. However, I know that sometimes you may feel like you don't have enough gas in the tank to be persistent, especially when you are stuck in a pit. So, allow me to let you borrow mine. This is one subject that I was persistent about. I may not have all of the answers in this area, but I sure know more now than I did back then. I genuinely hope that sharing this knowledge with you will be the boost you need to keep moving forward.

What I've found is that suffering always serves a purpose. Even when it seems senseless and evil, God can use that evil and turn it around for good. Sometimes suffering is meant to refine us. God will give us trials in order to teach us new lessons that will help to mature us, just as we use new challenges to teach our kids. I remember when my son was first learning to swim. He *hated* getting his face wet. With every swim lesson, I couldn't tell if there was more water on his face from the pool or his tears. And yet, there was a reason why I was sending him in to face this challenge despite his fear. In the long run, I knew that my son being able to swim would serve him well. It would be a skill that would not only keep him safe, but increase the amount of freedom and enjoyment he could have in the pool.

During the time that his swim lessons were taking place, I was going through a heavy amount of spiritual warfare. It seemed like every time I blinked, someone I loved was being admitted to the hospital, receiving emergency surgery, or being diagnosed with something. It got to the point where it felt too overwhelming. Naturally, I asked God why he was allowing me to go through such hardship. His response was simple, "Honey, just because your face is getting wet doesn't mean you're drowning." Ultimately, God used that season of constant sickness to teach me more about supernatural healing than I ever could've learned any other way. I learned how to seek God's will. I learned how to contend for God's best. I learned the power of prayer. And I learned to see God's heart in these situations, even when healing didn't come in the way I expected. See how that suffering served a purpose?

However, there are times when we seem to suffer for no good reason. Someone misuses their free will to use us or abuse us. Tragedy strikes. Trauma takes place. Fill in the blank. I'm sure you have a situation of your own that you could interject here. Can I just hold your heart for a minute? Those moments are not your fault. Nothing you did made you to blame for what happened to you. Sure, there may have been things that you could have done differently but that doesn't always guarantee a different outcome. That wasn't God's way of punishing you, either. What you experienced was just plain evil. We live in a fallen world. It happens to everyone.

In Matthew 5:45, it says, "He causes his sun to rise on the evil and the good, and sends rain on the righteous and the unrighteous." That means that we're all going to experience good things whether we deserve it or not, and we're all going to experience evil whether we deserve it or not. Why? Because God doesn't play favorites (Acts 10:34). If he were only able to bring people to repentance by bribing them with favoritism, then that wouldn't feel like much of a choice, would it?

Nevertheless, it's still indescribably painful when we have to walk through situations like this. But I can assure you of this—he's always going to be there to catch you and comfort you. When my little sister was just a toddler, she fell into the pool at a party. One minute she was toddling around the concrete, the next she was underwater. Before anyone could even scream, my dad dove into the pool, fully clothed, and scooped up his baby girl. Naturally, she was horrified. She coughed and screamed and sputtered as he carried her back to safety. And he held her as she cried.

You see, my sister didn't know that the pool could hurt her. As far as she could tell, it was a giant bathtub, what's the harm in that? She didn't have the knowledge or understanding to comprehend what would happen to her when she stepped off of that ledge. So, off she went, right into a death trap. Here's the interesting thing about that situation, though. My dad never scolded my sister for falling into the pool. He never blamed her for not knowing better. And he certainly didn't allow it to "teach her a lesson." She just wasn't yet mature enough to know how to follow her father's instruction. If she had been a little more mature, he could've warned her of the dangers of the pool and she could've chosen to heed his instruction. But she was just a child. And he understood that. He wasn't willing her to grow up faster, he was just holding her in that moment in time as she cried, meeting her with nothing but perfect love and understanding.

You may argue the point that if my dad had been all-knowing like God is, then he could've prevented anything bad from happening to her in the first place. And you'd be right. But even if that were the case, how could my sister know that my father was capable of saving her if there was never anything to save her from? How could she know that he was understanding enough to sit with her as she cried and not blame her for her own pain if she had never experienced what she went through that day? It may sound a little backwards (most things in the Kingdom of God usually do), but if God doesn't swoop in and prevent bad things from happening to us, I've found that it's usually because He wants to reveal more of His love to us in the aftermath.

Becoming a Victor

Victimhood can be a very tricky thing to find your way out of. Because it's one of those mindsets that leaves you feeling completely and utterly helpless. And when you feel helpless, it's easy to spend all of your time waiting for someone else to come and save you, growing more and more bitter by the day when it seems as though no one ever does.

So, how do you make it through this? I think the strategy is pretty simple. We have to remove the feeling of helplessness. We have to help you see how strong and secure you are right now. That approach is what's going to give you the power to rise above the temptation to wallow in self pity. The whole issue is that you feel as if there's nothing you can do. You don't realize how equipped you are right now, in this moment, to deal with everything you are facing.

You may have heard the phrase "God doesn't call the equipped, he equips the called." What that means is that whatever you have been called to, God will equip you to walk through. You don't have to be pre-qualified for God to give you everything you need to walk through this trial. Maybe you're walking through a struggle that is going to lead you closer to the calling God has placed on your life, or maybe you're suffering at the hands of someone else's carelessness. Either way, what is happening to you is not a surprise to God. That doesn't necessarily mean that He caused it to happen, but it does mean that He was prepared for any and all worst case scenarios.

Our family loves to take beach vacations. It's especially fun now that my kids are past the baby stage and can splash around in the tide pools while I sunbathe nearby. On one of these beach days in particular, there wasn't a cloud in the sky. I mean, the sun was blazing. And the bright sand didn't help with the reflection of the rays. Long story short, it was *extra bright* outside, and my son had forgotten his sunglasses. After several minutes of trying to push past his predicament, he couldn't take it anymore. He came to me crying. When I asked him what was wrong, he said, "Mama, my eyes hurt so bad. It's so bright outside and I forgot my sunglasses." Without saying a word, I reached into my bag and pulled out the sunglasses he so desperately needed. All of a sudden, he was perfectly equipped for the day and spent the next several hours splashing in every wave he could jump over.

You see, I had already packed everything I knew my son could possibly need. I had planned ahead. If it was sunny, I had his sunglasses. If he got hungry or thirsty, I had cold drinks and plenty of snacks. If we stayed at the beach for longer than anticipated, I had sunscreen. And backup sunscreen in case the first bottle ran out. None of these less-than-ideal conditions were going to catch me off guard. I was prepared for it all. But even as prepared as I was, I still can't see into the future. But God can. He knows exactly what storms lie ahead for you, and He's already prepared everything you're going to need when you get there. He has already packed everything you will need for the journey and nothing is going to take Him by surprise.

See, when I told you that story about my son's sunglasses, I told you that I had already provided my son with everything that he needed. So, how did he get what he needed? He brought the problem to me. My son didn't know what to ask for. He didn't know what things I had packed for him to solve his problems. All he knew was that he couldn't fix this on his own and he needed my help. And that was my cue to come in clutch with the provision. So many of us who struggle with victimhood spend our days squinting at the sun, complaining about how much our eyes hurt, rather than bringing the issue to our Father so that He can equip us with the very thing we need to overcome it.

Victory over Victimhood

Oftentimes, we are waiting for our circumstances to change before we can feel victorious. We want to taste victory before we've ever stepped foot on the battlefield. As much as I wish it were, that's just not the way life works. At least, not for those of us who follow Christ. Because that's not faith. In order for us to have faith, we have to be willing to step out and stand on that hope, even when we're a little uncertain of what the outcome will be.

Hebrews 11:1 says, "Now faith is confidence in what we hope for and assurance about what we do not see." We have to be confident in the things that we hope for. But in order to do that, we have to constantly remind ourselves that we serve a God who loves us and is always putting our best interests at heart. It is so, so easy to fall into the trap of thinking that because our situation feels hopeless, that must be evidence that God doesn't love us.

I recently heard an incredible quote, although I'm not sure who said it. But it's still impactful nonetheless. "Ships don't sink because of the water around them. They sink because of the water that gets in them." You see, our circumstances are not the problem. When we start letting our circumstances convince us that we are unloved, without hope, and beyond saving, that water is no longer surrounding us, it's getting inside of us and causing us to sink. Don't internalize your circumstances, friend. Don't allow yourself to think that the things that are happening to you are evidence that your Father doesn't love you. Bring your problems to Him. Ask Him for what you need, and He is faithful to equip you for anything that lies ahead.

Chapter Nine

Negativity

Every summer, my husband and I like to plant a garden. We spend the early weeks of spring prepping the ground, creating the rows, and planting the seeds. But as the summer months progress, the weather gets warmer and warmer. Actually, warm isn't the right word. It gets boiling hot in Mississippi. And I don't know about you, but I don't want to be in full sun in 100 degree heat for nearly an hour each day. I usually try to wait until the sun has gone beyond the trees before I go pick the vegetables, but if I do that, I typically only have time to pick the vegetables with no time left to tend to the weeds. Sure, I'll pick one or two as I go. I'll address the most aggressive weeds that are threatening to choke out the plants, but I don't stick around long enough to take care of all of them. Honestly, who has time for all of that?

A couple of summers ago, however, the weeds had become so overgrown in the garden that I couldn't even get in there to gather the food. I'm not sure what kind of invasive species was growing in the garden that summer, but the tall grasses were giving me an allergic reaction. For the rest of the season, my husband had to be the sole person in charge of collecting the vegetables. At that point, I was pretty bummed. I love gardening so much, but the fact that I hadn't kept the weeds in check meant that I was prevented from being able to enjoy the fruit of my labor. Or, in this case, the vegetables.

I've found that negativity works much the same way. We seem to have a tendency to think that we only have to deal with the worst of the weeds that try to choke out our positive thoughts. As long as we can still gather the crops, it's fine, right? The problem is that those weeds grow faster than the crops ever could. You could be one good storm away from those weeds overtaking your garden entirely. Listen, friend. If you want to get to the point where you are thriving, where you are not overtaken with crippling anxiety, worry, or stress, we've got to take care of those weeds.

Philippians 4:8 says, "Finally, brothers and sisters, whatever is true, whatever is noble, whatever is right, whatever is pure, whatever is lovely, whatever is admirable—if anything is excellent or praiseworthy—think about such things." Why do you think that we're supposed to focus on these things? Because whichever plant you water is the one that grows. If you water the weeds (your negative thoughts), they will grow. If you water the plants that produce fruit, more fruit will grow. Listen, I'm not telling you to just be happy and only think about the things that make you happy even when your life is absolutely crumbling around you. But it is possible to have your life crumbling around you and still be able to find God's hand at work in it.

As a kid, I used to watch a show called *Mr. Roger's Neighborhood.* Fred Rogers was one of those men who just seemed to be so full of light. Even on his children's show, he had a way of highlighting the good in the people and situations around him. Years later, when I became an adult, I saw an interview where he was talking about his mother inspiring him to have this sort of outlook on life. He said that whenever there would be times of chaos or crisis in the world, his mother would always tell him to "look for the helpers." He explained that whenever the world seemed to be falling apart, the helpers who came together to make everything right again were the ones who brought hope.

That's what I want you to see. Negativity will do nothing but steal the hope not only from you, but from everyone else around you. When you watch the news, you can either focus on the tragic house fire, or the firefighters who risked their lives to save those who were trapped. You can focus on the chaos, or you can focus on the ones who are doing everything in their power to make it right again. What you focus on really is up to you.

Check Your Lens

Now, I want you to understand that I am not talking about toxic positivity. I know that there are a lot of Christians out there who will tell you that happiness is a choice and that if you struggle with negative thoughts, you're doing it wrong. As if somehow your human nature makes you a bad Christian. That's not the angle I'm coming from here. Things in your life are going to suck. You're allowed to acknowledge that those things suck. I'm not asking you to pretend or shove down your feelings. What I am asking you to do is reevaluate your perspective.

My family and I recently went on a cruise. One of the ports we stopped in was Bimini, Bahamas. It was easily one of the most gorgeous places I have ever seen in my life. God's creativity is just never ending, isn't it? Of all of the gorgeous scenery, the water was by far my favorite part. It was so clear and blue, it legitimately looked like it had been photoshopped into the background of all of our pictures. I had never seen anything quite like it.

As my family was all sitting around admiring the views, I noted how the sepia toned sunglasses I was wearing made it look as if I was watching a movie. My sister-in-law asked if we could swap sunglasses for a minute so she could see things through my lenses. So I gave her my brown-tinted sunglasses and I put on her gray-tinted ones. All of a sudden, the colors that had been so vibrant a moment before were now dull and uninviting. Sure, the water was still gorgeous, but all of a sudden, it was much less appealing than it had been just a few moments before. Nothing about that scene had changed except for the lens that I was viewing it through.

Do you see my point? You may not be able to choose your circumstances. You might not have the ability at this current moment to change your financial situation or the status of your health. But what you do have within your control is your perspective. And the perspective or the "lens" through which you view your life can determine whether or not you actually enjoy the life you've been given.

One night, when my husband and I were still dating, we decided to go out to dinner. On this particular night, I was feeling a little bit agitated. It had been one of those days where everything seemed to be going wrong. Every little thing that had annoyed me throughout the day was piling up. And to make matters worse, the restaurant I really wanted to go to was closed, so we had to settle for another one nearby. Few things in this world make me more angry than deciding what I want to eat and not being able to eat it. Anyone else?

Anyway, once we got to this restaurant, there was a little bit of a wait. I took a seat on one of the benches and waited for them to call our names and seat us at a table. As I sat, simmering in my own irritation, a teenage boy came and took the seat beside me. He had thick glasses that indicated that he was struggling to see very well, and his set of forearm crutches were bearing most of his weight as he slowly eased his way onto the bench beside me. It seemed like even doing the most mundane tasks was a struggle for him.

After he caught his breath, he looked over at me with genuine eyes and asked, "How are you doing today?" It sounded like more than a simple question. It sounded as if he actually cared to know about my well-being. I appreciated his authenticity, but my foul mood still prevented me from wanting to engage in a deeper conversation, so I gave the typical, polite southern answer: "I'm fine, how are you?" Honestly, I expected the conversation to fizzle as it usually does when you follow the obligatory script. Instead, he turned toward me further and looked directly in my eyes. "I'm doing so great. I just got out of the hospital." My eyes widened in surprise. "You did?" I asked. "Yes, I have a terminal illness. I didn't think I would ever see the outside of that hospital building again. But I'm alive. And I'm getting to eat at a restaurant. I'm so happy to be here." Based on his body language and tone of voice, I could tell that he meant every last word.

There we sat, side by side. Two individuals coming to the same restaurant for the same thing, yet our perspectives were drastically different. I was mad that I wasn't getting what I wanted, and he was just happy to be there. One person was enjoying their life and the other was not. Now let me ask you this...which person do you think had more of a right to a negative outlook? Which one do you think has earned the right to be pessimistic about life? Spoiler alert, it wasn't me.

The one person in that room who had every right to be upset chose not to be. Why do you think that is? Maybe it was because staring death in the face had caused that young man to realize that life was too short to spend focusing on everything that was going wrong. He had been told that he didn't have much time left and he knew that he didn't want to waste it by focusing on things he couldn't control. He was determined not to let his circumstances steal his joy.

The thing is, none of us know with absolute certainty how much time we have left on this earth. We all just assume that we will make it to old age, but statistically speaking, that's not always the case. So let me ask you this. If you were diagnosed with a terminal illness tomorrow, would it change your perspective at all? Would you finally decide that you wanted to actually enjoy the rest of your days instead of putting joy off until tomorrow? Because here's the cold, hard truth. Your circumstances may never improve. In fact, on this earth, they could continue to get worse. And what if they do? Will you allow it to overtake you? Or will you take notes from that young man and actually enjoy the time you have left?

I don't know what happened to that boy. I never saw him again. I don't know if he beat his terminal illness or if, in the end, he succumbed to it. But I would bet my last dollar that if he did leave this earth, he enjoyed every last one of his days. All I want is for you to be able to say the same.

Being Realistic

Have you ever had a moment in your life where things start to go right for once and all of a sudden, you don't trust it? It's like the very things you hoped for are actually the things you fear the most. I'll tell you what I did when situations like that would happen. I would imagine all of the worst case scenarios that *could* happen, just so that I was prepared when the other shoe inevitably dropped.

If you've ever seen *Inside Out 2*, I'm sure you're at least somewhat familiar with the scene where Anxiety suppresses all of the main emotions and hijacks the dream factory so that they can imagine all of the mistakes Riley could possibly make. Anxiety justifies this by saying, "We need to be prepared!" Honestly, I used to justify my negativity the same way. What it all boiled down to is trust. Not only was I not trusting God with my future, I also didn't trust myself to be able to handle negative situations in the moment. Which is completely false.

When I was about 13 years old, my brother, my friend and I were all home alone while my parents were at work. My brother decided he was going to ride his bike down our secluded street. A few minutes later, he comes back into the house cradling his arm. "Call dad. I just broke my arm," he said. "Are you sure?" I asked. He moved his hand to reveal a bone protruding out of his elbow. "Yep, I'm pretty sure." At this point in my life, I had never seen a broken bone. The amount of blood and gore I had been exposed to was relatively low. My sweet friend that was with me nearly had a panic attack at the sight of the blood and bone. But me? I got to work. I sat my brother down on the couch, got him a pillow to rest his arm on, gave him some pain reliever and called my dad. I know that story is a little off topic, but what I'm trying to get you to see here is that anxiety has been lying to me for nearly all of my life.

Anxiety tried to tell me that I wasn't properly prepared for certain scenarios, that I couldn't trust myself to know what to do in those moments of conflict. Yet the story I just told you illustrates that I'm actually pretty dang good at taking care of people under pressure. Even at thirteen, I had the instinct to know what to do when an emergency arose.

All of this talk about "needing to be prepared" is bogus. Because even if you are the type of person who crumbles under pressure, you have a very real God who never will. I don't know if you've noticed, but there's a lot of high pressure scenarios in the Bible—and I mean *a lot.* And yet, I can't think of a single solitary verse that even implies that God is worried about any of it. He's the Alpha and Omega, Beginning and The End, Creator of all. Do you really think your financial situation is keeping Him up at night? Do you think He spends any length of time worried about your ongoing medical condition? No, because He's got it all figured out. You just have to trust that He actually knows what He's doing, and that He actually cares enough about you to fix it all in the end.

While anxiety is sitting there trying to predict what will happen, God already knows. And the thing is, anxiety is usually wrong. I can't tell you the amount of times I spent agonizing and preparing for situations that never actually happened. Trust me, friend. You're not "being realistic." You're being tricked into walking through life wearing a pessimistic lens. Thankfully, there is something you can do about it.

The Power of The Mind

Did you know that it is possible to literally rewire your brain? I'm serious. Way back when Paul wrote the book of Romans, he spoke about "renewing your mind." Now all these years later, science is finally starting to make sense of what he meant. Do you want to hear something wild? Your brain is hardwired to believe every single thing that it hears in your tone of voice. That means if you speak it enough, your brain will literally create new neural pathways, which is a physical manifestation of forming new beliefs.[1] For instance, let's say that you were to say to yourself, "The sky is purple" over and over and over and over. Eventually, your brain would actually start to believe it. Proverbs 18:21 says, "The tongue has the power of life and death, and those who love it will eat its fruit." God knew the way our brains worked before modern day science ever figured it out. So maybe it's time we start taking him at His word.

A friend of mine likes to say, "Your brain looks for evidence of what you speak." Meaning that if you are always saying that nothing good ever happens to you, guess what evidence your brain is going to start looking for? Imagine your brain working like a computer. If you go to a search engine and type in all of the different ways you could get cancer, what do you think that search engine is going to pull up? Do you think it's going to pull up all of the reasons why you shouldn't worry about it because it can't happen to you? No, a search engine pulls up only the information that's relevant to whatever you typed into the search bar. Our brains are meant to support us, not control us. So if you want to change your thoughts about your current reality, maybe you

---

1. Norman Doidge, The Brain That Changes Itself, on neuroplasticity and belief formation.

should change what you're "typing into the search bar," so to speak.

My husband taught me how to do this many, many years ago. You see, when we first started dating, I was absolutely riddled with insecurity. I was 17 years old and he was my first boyfriend. That was partially because I wasn't interested in dating just for fun, and part of it was because I didn't have very many people knocking on my door asking me out, if you know what I mean. But then Josh came along. And it was like he saw me when everyone else treated me like I was invisible. Even then, it was still a struggle for me to believe that I was actually worthy of someone like him. Remember, I spent the majority of my formative years believing there was something fundamentally wrong with me. So when Josh showed interest, I thought it was only a matter of time before he would find something he didn't like and walk away.

One day, he had had enough of my self-deprecation. Without saying a word, he took me into his bedroom where he had a full length mirror hanging on the back of his door. He placed me directly in view of the mirror as he stood behind me. "Look at her," he gently commanded. "Tell her you love her." It took me a good minute and a half to even get the words out. I had spent so long conditioning my brain to believe there was something wrong with the young woman standing in front of me that I could hardly stand to look at her, much less say anything good about her. He continued, "Now say, 'I am beautiful.'" Again, I choked out the words. He led me through a list of positive affirmations, guiding me to tell myself that I was a good person, that trying my best was enough, that I was loved and cared for.

I wish I could tell you that I walked away from the mirror that day feeling better. I didn't. In fact, I felt like a fraud and a liar. Because I didn't believe a single word I had just spoken over myself. It felt inauthentic. But every day, when I would visit Josh at his house, he would march me to that mirror and have me say those same words over and over again. After about a week, I started to wonder if maybe there was *some* truth to what I was saying. And after a few weeks, I was actually starting to believe it.

Listen, I know better than anyone what it's like to feel stuck in those old mindsets. You're probably thinking that if your body would change, you could love it more. Or that if people treated you better, you would be happier. Take it from me, there is nothing in your life that could change that would make you feel better if you don't learn how to be kind to yourself first.

I know I keep circling back around to the story of the Israelites, but it's because they are such a prime example of this. When they were in Egypt, they just wanted to be free. Once they were rescued, they started to wonder if life had been better in Egypt. They longed for the Promised Land, where they thought they could finally be happy, but once it was right in front of them, they refused to take it.[2] See, their circumstances kept changing but none of those changes ever made them any happier. In fact, it sounds like they became progressively more miserable to be

2. Exodus 14–16, New International Version.

around as time went on. Why? Because they never changed their stinkin' thinkin'.

Have you ever watched those shows about hoarders? I don't know what it is about those shows, but I find it fascinating to watch. I feel so deeply empathetic for these people who have suffered so much trauma that they literally find trash comforting. My heart breaks for the conditions that these people live in. Typically, in one of these shows, we get a good look at just how dire the person's circumstances are. Then a team of people will come in and clean the entire house out, and towards the end of the episode, we will get the reveal of the finished product with all of the drastic before and after photos that accompany it. I'm especially partial to the episodes that follow up with these people a few months later. Sometimes, they are able to keep it clean and habitable. But other times, the people go right back to hoarding the very trash that they had just been delivered from. Why is that? It's because they cleared out their home, but they never decluttered their mind. A change in their circumstances wasn't the solution to all of their problems.

Proverbs 26:11 says, "As a dog returns to its vomit, so fools repeat their folly." Now, I'm not saying these people are fools by any means. I think that if we were to take a good long look at our own lives, we could all point out places where we returned to things that we knew weren't good for us. But it does seem kind of silly doesn't it? To be rescued from something only to return to it later because it's familiar? I don't know about you, but I'm kind of tired of falling into that same old trap over and over again.

In order to combat this chokehold that negativity has on our lives, we have to be willing to do something different. Albert Einstein is believed to have said, "The definition of insanity is doing the same thing over and over again and expecting a different result." Which means, if we want a different result for our lives, we have to be willing to take a different approach. We can't keep entertaining all of these negative thoughts and expect for our lives to suddenly be positive and filled with joy. The change has to happen in the mind first.

There have been scientific case studies that measure the difference between cancer patients who have a positive outlook on their life versus those who had a negative or "realistic" outlook. These studies showed that the patients with a positive outlook increased their quality of life and reported a decrease in their pain levels as well as other undesirable side effects.[3] If this was done in an actual, measurable way through these studies, what do you think could happen to your life if you were to actually pursue those same changes on your outlook?

Victory over Negativity

In order to change your perspective, though, I'm going to have to ask you to do something that may be really difficult. I'm going to ask you to gather the courage to hope again. Listen, I un-

---

3. PubMed, "Study on Optimism and Quality of Life in Cancer Patients," 2023.

derstand how difficult that is. It's a big ask. Because it's scary. But I want you to hear me on this. If you are going through something difficult right now, it's because God trusts you to be able to handle it. He trusts that you will learn to trust Him through this because you are never alone. The latter half of Hebrews 13:5 says, "God has said, 'Never will I leave you; never will I forsake you.'"

Listen, these things that you're struggling with don't surprise Him. The issue is that you've been thinking that you're supposed to handle it on your own. That's why you're floundering. That's why you're thrashing around in the deep waters and feeling like you're drowning. Because you are. He never asked you to swim through this. Sometimes you just have to surrender to the process. Turn on your back and float. Let the water carry you to where you're meant to be. And part of surrendering to the process means allowing yourself to hope that everything will turn out the way it should.

Remember the movie *Finding Nemo*? Marlin, the overprotective pessimistic father, joins forces with Dory, the scatter-brained overly trusting sidekick, to find his son. At one point in the movie, they hitch a ride inside of a whale's mouth. Dory, who delusionally thinks she can communicate fluently with these whales, says that they need to go to the back of the throat. Marlin's mind snaps into worst-case-scenario mode. Dory tries to reassure him that everything is going to be alright. He replies with, "How do you know? How do you know something bad isn't going to happen?" To which she replies, "I don't."

See, the difference between Marlin and Dory is that Dory had hope. Was her life perfect and easy? No, not by any means. In fact, she seemed to get herself into some pretty tricky situations. But she enjoyed every last bit of it while Marlin was left floundering in his anxiety (pun intended). If we want to begin to break free from negativity, it's going to require us to have the courage to hope again.

Now, I will say that once you try to implement this, your brain will freak out at first. It's kind of like the first time you put a dog on a leash. They're used to having free reign of your property, so bringing them under submission comes with a bit of resistance. But if the dog is fighting against the leash, do you just let it go because training it is too hard? Or do you stick it out because you know that this level of obedience is what's best for you and the dog? Allowing yourself to hope will likely have the same results. At first, your brain will tug against that leash and try to convince you that this will never work. But once you're able to bring it under submission, not only will your quality of life improve, but it will likely impact everyone else around you as well.

I recently heard a quote at a church conference that I thought was absolutely beautiful. "Hope is borrowing tomorrow's joy for today." Hope is hard. I get that. Trust me, I do. But it is vital to living a fulfilled life. So if you're unable to find your hope for today, it's okay to reach into the future a little bit. Sunflowers seem to instinctively understand this principle. Throughout the day, sunflowers turn to face the sun, following it throughout the sky so that they can soak up as much light from it as possible. But what about when the sun sets in the west? That's when the sunflowers slowly turn towards the east, waiting for the sun to rise again. They seem to understand that darkness is temporary and that the sun will return as it always does. Don't let the darkness consume you, friend. Give yourself permission to hope that the light will return, and when it does, you will be positioned for it.

Chapter Ten

Fear

My husband has never flown on an airplane. And to be truthful, he doesn't want to. One day, as we were sitting around discussing our future, I shared with him how I wanted to travel and see different parts of the world, but that I wanted him to go with me. He said that he could find other ways to travel, by boat, by car, by train. Anything but an airplane. When I asked him why he was afraid, he replied, "I'm not afraid. I just don't like being in a form of transportation that I can't get out of if I need to. You can jump off a sinking ship or roll out of a moving car or train, but if you're in a pressure sealed tin can in the sky and something goes wrong, you're screwed." I chuckled a little to myself and said, "Listen, babe. I know you're not really familiar with this emotion so it's not easy for you to recognize it, but that's fear."

You see, my husband is not really afraid of anything. And he hasn't been in all the time that I've known him. He handles deadly voltages of electricity on a daily basis, for crying out loud. I have seen him walk across ceiling rafters above my head with no safety net, only a cold, concrete slab to land on if he were to fall. I've watched him manipulate a four-wheeler to rear back on two wheels and laugh while he did it. Fear is not in his vocabulary. And yet, here it was, creeping into our conversation so subtly that he wasn't even able to recognize it.

Fear has many forms, and some of them are so subtle that they are nearly undetectable to the untrained eye. Unlike Josh, I have always considered myself to be a fearful person. Growing up, I was always afraid of the dark, always saw danger in seemingly harmless situations, and–though I hate to admit it–a fateful incident with a giant balloon left me with a crippling distaste for loud noises of any kind. And even with all of those very obvious fears displayed for all to see, there were still some underlying fears that were much, much sneakier.

Yes, fear can look like we all think it will. Dread, anxiety, panic. But it can also look like worry, control, and manipulation. Anytime we try to determine the outcome of a certain situation in our lives, fear is usually the puppeteer behind our actions. It's sneaky. It's subtle. It comes in a whisper that sounds a lot like wisdom. It rarely shouts. It's control disguised as concern. And if we're not aware of what's happening, we can wind up being completely controlled by a force that we never agreed to.

I remember this happening to me just a few years ago. I had set a goal for myself to save up until I had a certain amount of money in my bank account. That's a good goal to have, right? I was being a good steward of the money God gave me. I wasn't spending it, I was saving it. What's wrong with that? The problem was that I was looking to that money for my security rather than God. And even though I could fool myself, I couldn't fool Him.

When I was *one* paycheck away from meeting my goal, I heard a very simple and very clear instruction. "Drain it." You want to talk about fear? I had been placing my sense of security in the amount of money I had in my bank account and with those two little words, God was asking me to face the thing I feared the most: trusting Him as my provider. Over the next few weeks, I did just as God asked. I became increasingly generous with the little nest egg that I had saved up. And do you know what I discovered? I love giving. I love taking care of people. I love making people feel seen. And fear had been stealing that from me. It caused me to put my trust in something other than God. That fear robbed me of the joy of just being God's child. But it didn't come in loudly, or forcefully. All it did was make tiny suggestions that sounded like the truth.

My son is and always has been a rule-follower. He also likes to understand how everything works. Honestly, he gets that part from me. So it's no surprise that when he hit three years old, the amount of questions he asked in a single day were innumerable. He was absolutely incessant. One thing in particular he was very interested in was how cars and roads worked. That part he got from his dad. He would ask questions about what gasoline is for, what each of the road signs said, and how we knew where to go every time we cranked the engine.

Once he had a bit of an understanding about how vehicles were meant to operate on the road, he became the world's tiniest backseat driver. "Daddy, how fast are you going? That sign said 45. You need to slow down or the cops are going to take you to jail." Or he would say, "Mommy, you're not supposed to go when it's a yellow light. Yellow means slow down, but you went faster." This went on and on and on until my husband finally told him that if he was going to be making all of those suggestions, he would need a back seat driver's license. And since my son is a rule follower, and he did *not,* in fact, have a back seat driver's license, he stopped making quite so many corrections.

I've noticed that fear sometimes seems to do the same thing. It's not actually driving the car, we are. But when we listen to all of the little tiny corrections it suggests, we may as well be handing over the keys. Fear can talk you into becoming so paranoid that you're checking your rear view mirrors more than the road ahead. It can make you so cautious that you keep your foot hovering over the brake rather than pressing the gas. Or worse, it can talk you out of driving to your destination entirely.

Think about it. When fear first entered this world, how did it happen? Way at the very beginning. Let's look at this story together in Genesis 3:1-12:

> Now the serpent was more crafty than any of the wild animals the Lord God had made. He said to the woman, "Did God really say, 'You must not eat from any tree in the garden'?" The woman said to the serpent, "We may eat fruit from the trees in the garden, but God did say, 'You must not eat

> fruit from the tree that is in the middle of the garden, and you must not touch it, or you will die.'" "You will not certainly die," the serpent said to the woman. "For God knows that when you eat from it your eyes will be opened, and you will be like God, knowing good and evil." When the woman saw that the fruit of the tree was good for food and pleasing to the eye, and also desirable for gaining wisdom, she took some and ate it. She also gave some to her husband, who was with her, and he ate it. Then the eyes of both of them were opened, and they realized they were naked; so they sewed fig leaves together and made coverings for themselves. Then the man and his wife heard the sound of the Lord God as he was walking in the garden in the cool of the day, and they hid from the Lord God among the trees of the garden. But the Lord God called to the man, "Where are you?" He answered, "I heard you in the garden, and I was afraid because I was naked; so I hid." And he said, "Who told you that you were naked? Have you eaten from the tree that I commanded you not to eat from?" The man said, "The woman you put here with me—she gave me some fruit from the tree, and I ate it."

Do you see what just happened? The enemy communicated to Eve by simply making a suggestive comment. He didn't shout. He didn't bully. He manipulated, ever so subtly. But it was enough to get Eve so far off track that she completely allowed it to control her actions. I want you to notice that the serpent didn't hand Eve the fruit. I think most of us picture this story almost like what happened in Snow White, where the evil witch is holding out the poisoned apple saying, "Take it, eat it." But that's not how this story unfolded. The serpent never offered Eve the fruit. He never even told her to eat it. He simply made a suggestive statement that planted a seed of doubt in what God had spoken to her, and then he sat back and watched it all play out.

If we want to keep fear from overtaking our lives, we have to learn how to deal with it. And that starts with being able to recognize it. I'm sure as you're reading this, you're probably already starting to recognize some of these patterns playing out in your own life. Maybe a situation has already come to your mind and you're starting to consider that maybe that was fear manipulating you after all. Hold that thought in your mind. That's the Holy Spirit talking to you, bringing things to your remembrance just like the Bible says in John 14:26. So now that you have that example locked and loaded, let's talk about what to do with it.

Fear vs Faith

First, we have to understand the difference between faith and fear. You might not think so, but they're actually pretty closely related. Why do you think fear is able to creep in so easily without being recognized? It's because it tugs at the same part of you that faith does. It draws you to look towards the future. The only difference is that fear often points to your past to make suggestions about the future. *You've struggled with finances your whole life. This new business venture is probably going to turn out the same way.* That's how fear speaks. *You've had so many negative pregnancy tests, what makes you think this one will be positive?* All of a sudden, these suggestions about your past–which are true–lead you to believe that fear understands your future. It doesn't.

Isaiah 43:19 says, "See, I am doing a new thing! Now it springs up; do you not perceive it? I am making a way in the wilderness and streams in the wasteland." If God is constantly doing new things in our lives and calling new things forth in our circumstances, why is it that we are so tempted to cling to our past? I'll tell you why. It's because the enemy loves to speak to what we've already experienced. He uses those things as evidence to support his argument. Faith requires us to believe in the Creator, not the recycler.

You see, the enemy can't create anything new. His only option is to recycle what's already been done in the past. So the fact that he keeps bringing up your past is just evidence that he is unimaginative. God, on the other hand, creates new things all the time. He creates them out of absolutely nothing. He is not limited in the ways He can grow and adapt and mold your future into something that is completely unrecognizable to you. I've watched Him do it in my own life time and time again. That doesn't mean your past is wasted, sometimes He can use what's happened to you in the past and breathe new life into it.

One of my favorite things to do is watch renovation shows. There's something so therapeutic about watching an old house be given a second chance. If I were to ever move from where I'm currently living, I would not want to build something new from scratch. Give me an old building with loads of character. The older and quirkier, the better. Now, that's probably ironic for me to say because my dad made an entire career of constructing new homes from the ground up. I watched the process of something being built from nothing. I can't tell you how many home construction sites I've been on and how many builder-grade homes I've helped clean. One thing I learned from watching renovation shows of existing homes and first-hand experience of new builds is that the past and the future can coexist in a beautiful way.

If you've ever watched one of those shows where they renovate a super old home, you've probably seen them run into a ton of issues that have to be dealt with, one of which is cast iron pipes. Back in the day, they used to use cast iron pipes in all of the plumbing fixtures. While it is a strong, durable material, the one problem they didn't foresee was the erosion of the cast iron over time. I don't know if you know this, but plumbing pipes don't work super efficiently when there is a giant hole rusted through them. So oftentimes, in these shows, they will have to remove the old pipes entirely and run new ones. Why? Because the old method wasn't working anymore.

The same is true in our lives. Those old methods from your past might not be working anymore, so it would make sense that God would want to do a new thing, right? But that doesn't mean the entire house has to be demolished. God can work with the existing structure of your past and give it new life, just like they do on those home renovation shows. We're just hesitant to believe this because we think that our past disqualifies us from what God is trying to do in our lives. We believe that somehow we are broken beyond repair. That the only way our lives can be useful is if they're torn down entirely. But I don't know if you've noticed, Jesus is pretty handy at fixing things. He was a carpenter, after all.

We see him doing this very thing in the story of the woman at the well. She had a past, and a pretty damaged one at that. Jesus knew this, but He didn't shy away from her. Instead, He leaned in. Watch what happened in John 4:39, "Many of the Samaritans from that town believed in Him because of the woman's testimony, 'He told me everything I ever did.'" Jesus took an isolated, heartbroken woman searching for love in all of the wrong places and gave her a different future as one of the first evangelists.

You see, fear and faith both require the same thing from us. They both require us to believe something that hasn't happened yet. Faith requires us to believe that God is capable of restoring our past and using it to create something new. Fear, on the other hand, tries to get us to believe that our past is an indicator that nothing will ever change. That we are just an old, broken building with rusted pipes and that's all we'll ever be. But fear hasn't met the right carpenter.

Victory over Fear

I recently heard an incredible analogy about how fear works in our minds. Have you ever seen videos of circus elephants? Listen, I'm not condoning the methods that are used for training these animals. For the sake of this analogy, I just need you to understand that these massive elephants are able to be trained by humans. How does that happen? You have these incredibly powerful creatures that are bowing in submission to a person that they could easily crush beneath their feet.

Fear moves in a similar pattern. We can combat it if we have the courage to recognize our authority and stand up against it, and yet we allow ourselves to be pushed around by something that Jesus already defeated. Courage is not the absence of fear, it's the ability to feel the fear and do it anyway. Several times in the Bible, God commanded His people not to be afraid. Why would He say that if that was something they were incapable of doing? Isaiah 41:10 says, "So do not fear, for I am with you; do not be dismayed, for I am your God. I will strengthen you and help you; I will uphold you with my righteous right hand." Yes, this verse is a reminder that we shouldn't be afraid, but it's also a solution to the problem of fear. God's solution is to remind the people of who He is.

Whenever we are being bombarded with thoughts of fear (because we all are, at some point or another), one of the ways we can buck against it is by reminding ourselves of who God is. In my first book, *7 Days to a Life of Limitless*, I shared the story of my dog, Chewy. Chewy was an answered prayer and two months after we got him, he was tragically hit and killed by one of my neighbor's cars. Not to mention that this was directly following an incident where a coyote attacked and killed nearly all of our chickens. Needless to say, the safety of my animals became a big source of fear for me during that time. Then one day, I stumbled across this verse. Psalm 36:6, "Your righteousness is like the highest mountains, your justice like the great deep. You, LORD, preserve both people and animals."

From that point on, anytime I would feel the fear or concern about my animals safety begin to rise, I would repeat that verse to myself over and over. *You, Lord, preserve both people and animals. You, Lord, preserve both people and animals.* Over time, the fear began to dissipate because I wasn't giving it a foot in the door. I was demanding to see its backseat driver's license and it couldn't produce one. The more I repeated that verse to myself, the more my brain started to actually remember how faithful God is. This is exactly what I believe Paul is talking about in Romans 12:2 when he says to "be transformed by the renewing of your mind." But we can't expect it to happen automatically. We have to be willing to put in the work and stick with it. Fear doesn't leave on its own, it has to be evicted.

I've talked about how my dad used to be involved in construction and real estate. He's dabbled in a little bit of everything. Site design, landscaping, building, flipping, and even rental properties. Sometimes, situations arise in rental properties where the landlord has to ask the tenants to leave. And if you believe that those tenants graciously leave the very first time they are asked, you would be very wrong. Sometimes the authorities have to get involved. Sometimes they leave kicking and screaming. Sometimes there is a giant mess to be cleaned up afterwards. But just because evicting the fear is a difficult process doesn't mean it should be allowed to stay. Sometimes, you're the one who has to dig your heels in, stand your ground, and square off with the very fear that is trying to take you down. It may be difficult, but it's not impossible. Remember what Matthew 19:26 says? "With man this is impossible, but with God all things are possible."

Chapter Eleven

Lonliness

There is a profound difference in being alone and feeling lonely. Just because you are by yourself, doesn't mean you're lonely. Anyone can learn to be perfectly content with their own company, but loneliness is a different monster entirely, and one I am all too familiar with. Because when you're lonely, there's a deep sadness attached to it, like a monkey on your back that you just can't seem to shake. You watch other people live their lives with their friends and family, perfectly happy and content while you struggle in silence. It's a feeling of being overlooked. Of feeling like your problems don't matter to anyone else. You may even feel like your very existence is of little consequence to those around you. I've been there. And it's not a fun place to be. But because I've been there, I can tell you that it won't always be this way.

We serve a God of order. There is a process to every single thing that He does. He's not a magic genie that zaps things into existence. Even if we don't want to admit it, we all have a tendency to think that way. Just look at creation. He spoke, and it appeared.

Seems pretty simple, right? Okay, so let me challenge that idea for a second. If there is no process and God is able to just speak things into existence on a whim, then why didn't He create every single thing in one day? In one breath? Why did He feel the need to stretch it out over a period of seven whole days? (Or, technically six if you don't count the rest day). It's because there was a process. There's always a process.

Let's take a deeper look at the creation process, because I really think this is going to help you in your own life. Let's read through Genesis 1:1-26 together:

> In the beginning God created the heavens and the earth. Now the earth was formless and empty, darkness was over the surface of the deep, and the Spirit of God was hovering over the waters. And God said, "Let there be light," and there was light. God saw that the light was good, and he separated the light from the darkness. God called the light "day," and the darkness he called "night." And there was evening, and there was morning—the first day. And God said, "Let there be a vault between the waters to separate water from water." So God made the vault and separated the water under the vault from the water above it. And it was so. God called the vault "sky." And there was evening, and there was morning—the second day. And God said, "Let the water under the sky be

gathered to one place, and let dry ground appear." And it was so. God called the dry ground "land," and the gathered waters he called "seas." And God saw that it was good. Then God said, "Let the land produce vegetation: seed-bearing plants and trees on the land that bear fruit with seed in it, according to their various kinds." And it was so. The land produced vegetation: plants bearing seed according to their kinds and trees bearing fruit with seed in it according to their kinds. And God saw that it was good. And there was evening, and there was morning—the third day. And God said, "Let there be lights in the vault of the sky to separate the day from the night, and let them serve as signs to mark sacred times, and days and years, and let them be lights in the vault of the sky to give light on the earth." And it was so. God made two great lights—the greater light to govern the day and the lesser light to govern the night. He also made the stars. God set them in the vault of the sky to give light on the earth, to govern the day and the night, and to separate light from darkness. And God saw that it was good. And there was evening, and there was morning—the fourth day. And God said, "Let the water teem with living creatures, and let birds fly above the earth across the vault of the sky." So God created the great creatures of the sea and every living thing with which the

> water teems and that moves about in it, according to their kinds, and every winged bird according to its kind. And God saw that it was good. God blessed them and said, "Be fruitful and increase in number and fill the water in the seas, and let the birds increase on the earth." And there was evening, and there was morning—the fifth day. And God said, "Let the land produce living creatures according to their kinds: the livestock, the creatures that move along the ground, and the wild animals, each according to its kind." And it was so. God made the wild animals according to their kinds, the livestock according to their kinds, and all the creatures that move along the ground according to their kinds. And God saw that it was good. Then God said, "Let us make mankind in our image, in our likeness, so that they may rule over the fish in the sea and the birds in the sky, over the livestock and all the wild animals, and over all the creatures that move along the ground."

Do you see the order of development here? God had to create the sky, the land and the sea first, otherwise the plants would have nowhere to be rooted, no air to sustain them, and no light to help them grow. He had to create the fish and the birds to distribute nutrients before the land could sustain other creatures. And he had to create everything before he created man, otherwise man would have nothing to have dominion over. See the pattern?

So if God is so intentional, so orderly, and so precise with the creation of the universe, what makes you think He would do things differently in your own life? What makes you think He's going to zap you with everything you need all at once? Make no mistake, He will give you everything you need, but sometimes you have to go through His process to get it. God doesn't zap us with growth, He walks us through it.

You wouldn't put a whole egg, a handful of flour and baking soda into a bowl, pop it into the oven and expect to get a cake, would you? You understand that the ingredients have to be prepared, sifted, and mixed before the batter will even form. And you understand that the batter has to be transferred to the right container to be able to withstand the heat. And you understand that the baking process takes time, over consistent exposure to high temperatures in order for that batter to become what it was intended to be. So what makes you think God isn't doing the same for you?

God isn't allowing you to go through this because He doesn't love you. He loves you too much to rush this process. He is so careful with you because He wants this development process to turn out just right. Just like with baking, if you rush through the process, there's a chance that it won't turn out right and you may have to start all over, which takes even more time. God's not going to do that to you. He's not going to allow you to move forward until this part of the process is complete. But rest assured, you're not intended to be here forever. But since you are here right now, let's reframe the way you think so that withstanding the heat will become that much easier.

Isolation or Incubation?

Here on our little makeshift farm, we love to hatch chickens. There's something so fascinating about taking an ordinary egg and watching it slowly develop into a living, breathing creature. Every time we hatch a batch of eggs, I can't help but wonder what that must feel like for the baby chicks. The bigger they grow, the more cramped and uncomfortable their environment becomes. It's not like a human baby that's developing inside of a womb that can stretch. Those baby chicks are inside of a fixed shell. If they get a cramp and want to stretch their legs, they're out of luck. The only way to get out of the discomfort is to break free from that shell.

I think that's how seasons of isolation can feel for us sometimes. All we know is that it's dark, lonely, and uncomfortable. What we don't see is that we're being prepared for a level of freedom that we've never known before. God's not isolating you, He's incubating you. You're not being put in this position for no reason. You've been put through this temporary season in order to prepare you for much, much more.

Back in 2019, I went through a season of so much loss. One of our family members lost a large home where we used to gather together. All of a sudden, there were no more family Thanksgivings, no more lake days, no more projects to work on all together. While we were still a large family that loved each other, we no longer had a place to meet up and prove it.

A few months later, I lost my dog to lymphoma. I know, some people say, “It’s just a dog, it’s not like you lost a family member.” But in my mind, this dog was my family. Bruce had been with me through the most traumatic years of my life up to that point. He had calmed me through my most intense battles with PTSD. He gave me a reason to get out of bed during my years of depression. He was always there to protect me when I didn’t trust myself enough to protect myself. So, no, he wasn’t just a dog. He represented a constant source of comfort and encouragement to keep going when everything in me was screaming that I should give up.

And of course, we all know what followed 2019. 2020. The year that the entire world lost its mind. It might not have been so bad if I hadn’t just gone through some of the hardest losses of my life. But not only did I have to suffer through everything 2020 threw at us collectively, September of that year was also when I lost my grandmother to dementia and found out my dad had cancer. All within the same week. Oh yea, and my husband was also out of town for work during that time. You want to talk about an uncomfortable season? It was torturous. It wasn’t just loneliness I was feeling. It was perpetual defeat coupled with the fact that, because of my isolation, no one on the outside seemed to notice that I was drowning.

And yet, looking back now, I can see the process of what God was doing, even in the loss. You see, September of that year was when my egg finally cracked. I couldn't take it inside that shell anymore. I had to break free. That was the season where I fully found God and started walking out a real relationship with Him. If I had not been completely alone when I got the news of my dad's diagnosis, I never would've cried out to God. If Bruce had still been alive, I would have instinctively reached to him for comfort. If our family had still had our gathering place, I might've tried to run away from my problems and into the arms of my family instead. And if I had not suffered through all of that loss, all of that pain, and all of that torment, you would not be reading this book right now. I never would have learned to hear God's voice, so I never would've learned all of the things He's taught me. I never would've heard him tell me to get on Tiktok and share what I was learning, or to write my first book, or the book you're reading right now. It was all a process of development. And it was all meant for my good.

Listen, I'm not saying you'll never struggle. You will. You can expect that. But what I am saying is that when you struggle, there is purpose behind it. Look for the purpose, and you will find the reason to keep fighting and the will to break free.

It reminds me of the story of Elijah. In 1 Kings 17, God tells Elijah to tell King Ahab some bad news. Elijah tells Ahab that because of his disobedience to God, a drought is about to hit the land. King Ahab is unsurprisingly angry at this declaration. So once Elijah leaves Ahab's presence, God sends him to a place of complete and total isolation. Or was it incubation? He sends him to a small little brook called Cherith. While Elijah is there, he's downright uncomfortable. There's no bed, no food, and no company of any kind. To make matters worse, God provides for Elijah by having ravens bring him food. At that time, ravens were considered an unclean animal. And, honestly, I'd have to agree. I don't know about you, but I've watched nature documentaries. I've seen how birds feed their babies. They digest the food, regurgitate it, and spit it into their babies mouths. Gross. And now you're telling me that the same beak that feeds their baby birds that way is now going to be touching the food that I am expected to eat? No thank you. I'd rather starve.

I think Elijah understood better than anyone what it was like to be in an uncomfortable season. And the worst part is that he didn't know when it would end. Some commentators believe he wound up staying at that brook and being fed by those nasty ravens for around eighteen straight months. Can you imagine? I'll bet he woke up everyday thinking *maybe this will be the day when God finally gets me out of here.* And yet, everyday, he was disappointed. For eighteen months. But what Elijah gained during that season was far more important than everything he gave up.

In that season, Elijah learned how to have a deep dependence on God. You see, being at the brook gave him experiential faith. Elijah didn't just know that God was his provider in theory, he *experienced* it every day for eighteen months. Elijah didn't just hear God's voice occasionally. I'd be willing to bet that he talked to God all day everyday for a solid eighteen months. How else would he be able to keep from going crazy? He experienced what it was like to have conversations with God every single day during that season. And having that deep, deep connection with God was what served him well in the years to come.

See, a lot of us say that we believe God is our provider, but how many of us have actually been put in a position where we've had to experience it first hand? Many of us say that we talk to God, but how many of us are stopping long enough to listen to what He wants to say back? If you've been put in a season of isolation, you're not here by accident. You're here because God is drawing you into a deeper relationship with Him. You're here because He's trying to make it easier for you to find Him. He's removing all of the blockages that kept you from getting to Him before and that is a gift. But just like any other gift, you have to actually open it before it can ever be useful to you.

Listen, I know it's hard. I know that you are struggling with just how uncomfortable it all is. At times, I'm sure you even feel like you're suffocating. That just means you're that much closer to discovering parts of your Father's love that you've never known before. You are in position. And when the time is right, you will hatch.

Do you want to know what else is cool about hatching chickens? Once the first one breaks out of the egg, the others quickly follow suit. Do you know why that is? It's because their chirps communicate to each other when it's time to break free. Once a chick still inside of its shell hears the peeps and movements of the others who have made it out, they are more encouraged to do the same. Let me be that person for you. Let me be the one to tell you that I have been through that season of incubation (for *years*, in fact). And I can confidently say that every bit of discomfort was worth it. Every struggle equipped me. Every challenge refined me. But I made it out, so I know you can, too. And one day, your testimony of how you broke free from that season will be exactly what someone else needs to hear so they can get out, too. You are not alone, you're just lonely for now. But trust me when I say that the blessing on the other side of it will make every bit of the heartache worth it.

A Different Kind of Discomfort

Okay, let's go back to the butterfly analogy from the beginning of this book for a second. There's one very important part of the process that I want you to see, so stick with me. It's the part that happens when the butterfly is ready to emerge from isolation, but isn't quite ready to fly. It's the moment where everything shifts. This is the point where the butterfly emerges from its chrysalis. This part of the process is actually pretty fascinating. The butterfly has this instinctual understanding of when it has developed enough to emerge into the next step of the process. It will then tear a hole in the chrysalis using its "claws" on its legs. All of this movement triggers the release of a chemical that causes its wings to expand. From that point, the butterfly has a few minutes to fight its way out of the chrysalis before it gets stuck. Doesn't sound too fun does it? But here's the fascinating part. If the butterfly didn't have to go through this struggle, its wings wouldn't have the strength to fly. Resistance always leads to growth. This whole process is a necessary orchestration that equips the butterfly with everything it needs for the next step on its journey.

Being cramped inside of that small cocoon that's growing more uncomfortable by the day doesn't sound like a fun place to be. But having to fight for your life to escape before your wings inflate like a balloon and trap you there doesn't sound much better, does it? As much as I hate to tell you this, every step of your journey is going to be uncomfortable. Each and every time you have to take a leap of faith, it's going to feel a little bit scarier than last time. But it's all by design, to equip you for what's next.

We see this happening in Elijah's story, too. In Elijah's case, (and maybe in yours, too), that season of isolation was preparing him for community. And his community prepared him for his calling. In 1 Kings 17, God sends Elijah on a new adventure. Once the brook at Cherith dries up, God commands him to go to a town called Zarephath where he is to stay with a widow and her son. Back in that time, widows really had no way to provide for themselves. Women were solely dependent on their husbands to make sure they had food, clothing, and shelter. So if their husband died and they were unable to find another, they were sort of out of luck. That's exactly what we see happening with this poor woman. When Elijah finds her, she is out collecting sticks for a fire so that she can cook her son one last meal before their provision completely runs out.

I can't help but wonder what Elijah must be thinking at this moment. He's just come from a place of complete isolation. I'm sure he probably prayed every day for God to give him some sort of company. He probably imagined what it would be like to have a family again, to sleep on a bed again, to have a conversation again. And here he is, being led to stay with a woman who doesn't have much more to offer than where he just came from. Yet again, he is being asked to get uncomfortable, just in a different way this time. Same season, different font.

But make no mistake, this wasn't to punish Elijah, it was simply the next level of preparation. See, this widow needed Elijah. And Elijah needed her. If Elijah had not just seen God provide for him day after day, he wouldn't have been able to impart that level of faith into this widow that God could provide for her too. If she hadn't allowed him to stay with her, Elijah would've missed out on some of the lessons that prepared him for Mount Carmel.

The thing is, even these pairings are strategic. Nothing about the community you're going to step into will be random. If it's truly where God is leading you, there will be complimentary people waiting for you on the other side. In the animal kingdom, these are called symbiotic relationships. One of the simplest examples of this is the clownfish and the anemone. Their partnership is mutually beneficial. The stinging anemone provides protection from predators, as well as a safe breeding ground for the clownfish. But the anemone benefits from the clownfish's ability to remove parasites, protect from predators, and water and nutrient circulation. In short, they both help each other grow. There isn't just one party benefitting more heavily from the other. They work together in perfect harmony. No matter where you're headed, you can guarantee that the people in your future will have something you need. And chances are, you will have something they need in return.

As I'm writing this, this subject is resonating so deeply with me because I literally just walked through it. You see, I had been in a season of isolation for a very long time. For five solid years, it was just me and God. Along the way, he blessed me with several long distance friendships that are still important to me to this day, but on a daily basis, my only constant source for communication was God himself.

Then one day, out of nowhere, he asked us to move churches. We had been going to church with my husband's family about an hour away from where we live. Our church was filled with wonderful people who loved us, plus, we got to spend time with family every single week, but the distance kept us from being able to get heavily involved. In all honesty, we had no good reason to leave. All we knew was that God said it was time to get local, and we had to choose to obey him even when it didn't seem to make much sense. We started attending a church about 15 minutes from our home, and for the first six months or so, we were just trying to get a feel for it. Then one Sunday morning, the pastor stopped by to talk to us, which wasn't unusual, but this time was different. He didn't just make small talk or tell us it was good to see us. He started asking questions about our lives, about what led us here, about our story. He got invested in us, which was something that I had not seen very many pastors do.

A little while later, he invited us to start coming to their small group. And so we did. That was when I realized just how uncomfortable God was asking me to become. Week after week, I started to fall more and more in love with the people at our new church. They would make simple little comments in passing that would heal heart wounds that I didn't even know I still had. And I became terrified.

As I was praying about it one night, God gave me a vision to help me understand why this part of the process was so necessary for my growth. In this vision, I was standing in the pastor's home during a small group night. Jesus and I were off in a corner whispering to each other. I said, "Jesus, why do I have to do this? It's been you and me for the past five years and I thought we had a good thing going. I've learned so much when it's been just the two of us. Why does it have to change?" What I was really saying is *these people are scary. They love me too well and it terrifies me to my core.* Jesus simply replied, "I'm not leaving you, but it's time you learned what it feels like to be loved by your own kind."

All of a sudden, through these people, God's word started to come to life. I started to understand Psalm 68:6, "God sets the lonely in families." He wasn't setting me into a physical family to meet my physical needs. He was placing me in a spiritual family to meet my spiritual needs. He was showing me what it looks like for people to actually be the hands and feet of Jesus. To love one another well, to hold each other's pain, and to stick around when things get messy.

In the isolation, God had healed me of my need for other people's validation, but in this new season, he was healing me of the rejection wound that had plagued me my entire life. If he had launched me into this church before the need for validation had been removed, I would've become codependent. But if he had elevated me before walking me through this season of healing through restorative relationships, the weight of that elevation would've caused me to crumble. Each and every part of the puzzle is necessary in order to create the bigger picture.

I don't know what wounds you struggle with. I don't know what circumstances you need to heal from, but what I do know is that there is a process God is taking you through. The isolation is going to strip you of everything you don't need. The community is going to heal the things you didn't know were still broken. And it's all a set up for a bigger purpose that's coming.

Community Prepares Us for Calling

One of the most famous parts of Elijah's life story is the story of what happened at Mount Carmel (1 Kings 18). After Elijah left the widow's house, he was sent to face the prophets of Baal and Asherah on Mount Carmel and challenge them to a biblical duel. There were 850 false prophets in all, and only one Elijah. Oh, and did I mention that literally all of Israel was there to watch it all unfold? Talk about pressure. Somehow, it didn't seem to rattle

Elijah. He did exactly what God called him to do. He gave the false prophets a chance to call down fire from heaven, which they could not. And then, he stacked the odds against himself by having his altar soaked with water three different times. At that point, he said a simple prayer, and stepped back so God could do his thing. And boy, did he. God sent fire from heaven that soaked up all of the water, burned the offering, and even melted the stones. Everyone in attendance was amazed at God's awesome display of power.

See, we all want the Mount Carmel moments. We often want God to show up in our lives and use us in these big, extravagant ways. But most of us aren't willing to do what Elijah did to get what Elijah got. Remember, he had been in hiding for three years at this point. For three years, no one recognized him. His name wasn't being passed around in circles of influence. He wasn't being seen or acknowledged for what he was doing. But that didn't make what he was doing any less essential for where God was leading him.

What we often gloss over is how the moments at the widow's house helped to prepare him for exactly what he was going to experience on Mount Carmel. At one point, the widow's son became sick and died. She was absolutely distraught, as any mother would be. In her anger, she blames Elijah for what happened. I want you to see what Elijah does next, because it's a really important piece of the story. Let's read 1 Kings 17:19-24.

> "Give me your son," Elijah replied. He took him from her arms, carried him to the upper room

> where he was staying, and laid him on his bed. Then he cried out to the Lord, "Lord my God, have you brought tragedy even on this widow I am staying with, by causing her son to die?" Then he stretched himself out on the boy three times and cried out to the Lord, "Lord my God, let this boy's life return to him!" The Lord heard Elijah's cry, and the boy's life returned to him, and he lived. Elijah picked up the child and carried him down from the room into the house. He gave him to his mother and said, "Look, your son is alive!" Then the woman said to Elijah, "Now I know that you are a man of God and that the word of the Lord from your mouth is the truth."

I love this part of the story. This is such a pivotal point in Elijah's journey. This is the first recorded resurrection we have in the Bible. Elijah would've had no way to even know that this was possible. All he knew was that he cared about this boy and his mother, and he had developed a close enough relationship with God to have the courage to ask for the impossible. And God delivered. As amazing as this story is, do you see how even this was preparation for where Elijah was headed? When he got to Mount Carmel, he had to have the courage to once again ask God to do the impossible. Except this time, he had to do it in front of an entire nation. But because he had seen God come through before, he had the faith that God would do it again.

Not long ago, I had an encounter with a widow of my own. Our church recently purchased a new building that they are renovating in order to hold more people. Occasionally, they will have work days to clean up the new building and prepare it for renovations. On one of those days, I went to help. As I started cleaning, a lady came up and started helping me. She introduced herself as one of my friend's moms. As we began working, she started to tell me about her recent battle with breast cancer and all of the complications that came with her recovery. Keep in mind that I had just come from a season of heavy isolation (incubation). I had been alone with my kids all day every day for the past five years. Of course, my husband was there too, but with his grueling work schedule, I was lucky to get more than a few hours a day with him. I had almost forgotten how to have a conversation with another adult. I had forgotten what it felt like to sit with someone and listen to their story. Listening to this woman share her pain was such a breath of fresh air to me. Suddenly, all of the love that God had been pouring into me for the past five years had somewhere to go.

Here's the thing, though. There were no fireworks. I did not have a massive word of knowledge about her situation. I don't even recall saying anything remotely groundbreaking to this woman. All I did was acknowledge how hard that must have been, share that I understood her pain because of similar experiences with my dad, and tell her how strong I thought she was. Literally, this woman was working circles around me. That day, we went our separate ways, both feeling filled up by our shared experience. And I didn't think about it again.

Fast forward a couple of months; I started leading a small group at my church. It was one of the most rewarding experiences of my life. No, it wasn't theatrical. Miracles didn't break out and people didn't get miraculously healed. But we did see the chains start to fall off of them one by one. I had a front row seat to watch them be reshaped by their Father's love, and it was absolutely beautiful. By the end of the small group, we began reflecting on our time together and encouraging each other. The woman that I had worked with at the work day had joined my group, and she spoke up. She shared how she had not regularly attended our church before that day. She shared how she had never joined a small group before because she never felt like she belonged. But on that day when we worked together, her conversations with me and one other woman made her feel seen. She started attending our church, coming to Bible study on Wednesday nights, and joined my small group all because of that one day. That one seemingly insignificant conversation made her feel more seen than I may ever know.

In that moment, I wasn't watching someone's physical body being resurrected from the dead, but I was watching someone's heart being brought back from the brink of rejection. I watched her settle into her identity as a child of God, who was loved and accepted into his family. Watching that make such an impact in her life made a big impact in mine as well. The reality is, I'm still very much in the middle of this process. I know that there is much more to come and that I am nowhere near done learning. There is so much of God that I have yet to experience. There are so many pieces of Him that have yet to be revealed to me. But I am confident that I am exactly where I am supposed to be at this point in the process.

Here's another piece I've noticed about Elijah's story. When most people think of Mount Carmel, they think of the fireworks (literally). They think about the great display of God's power. And don't get me wrong, that is super cool. If I ever experienced literal fire falling from heaven, I would probably pass out from excitement. But what most people miss is not *what* God did but *why* He did it. He did it because of his love for his people. Elijah wasn't sent to Mount Carmel just to roast his enemies (pun intended). He was sent there to rescue the people. God had a heart, first and foremost, to see these people restored to him. He wasn't trying to prove himself to the false prophets, he was revealing himself to his kids. And Elijah couldn't have been a part of that if he hadn't spent time among them.

Something else you need to understand about Elijah's stay with the widow is where she was located. Zarapheth was pagan country. Idol worship was rampant in this part of town. Not to mention, Zarapheth is right next door to the town where Jezebel (Elijah's arch nemesis) was raised. He was quite literally in enemy territory. Why do you think God sent him there? Of all places, why would God send one of his most dedicated prophets to a region that is practically run by the enemy? My theory is that God did that because he needed to develop Elijah's compassion for those people.

You don't get to the point where you're calling fire down from heaven until you put in the time among the people you're meant to set free.

Again, this part of the process usually doesn't happen quickly. Yes, God can make things happen in an instant, but when we're talking about something that is going to bring an entire nation back to his arms, that's something that takes time to set up. This isn't just a flash in the pan. The bigger the calling is on your life, the higher the chances are that your preparation will take longer. You have to be stripped of everything you don't need and equipped with everything you do. So, no, it won't be fast, but the preparation is absolutely necessary.

Victory over Loneliness

I'm guessing that at this point in your journey, you haven't quite made it to Mount Carmel yet. That's okay, I haven't either. No matter where you are in the process–whether you are in that season of incubation, or God has led you into your community–you are exactly where you need to be. Whenever we are stuck in those seasons of loneliness, it's so easy to get trapped in the idea that nothing will ever change. We often think that we are doomed to be alone forever. Loneliness is just one checkpoint along the journey. It is not your destination. I want you to remember that good things take time to grow. This isn't going to happen overnight.

The one thing that we have to remain mindful of is that God has something to teach us in each chapter of our lives. If you are still stuck in the same place you've been in for years, it's because you still have more to learn before you can move on. Think about it like school. You can't move on to middle school until you've successfully completed everything you needed to learn in elementary. And you can't move on to high school until you've completed middle school. Trust me, God is the best teacher there is. He knows exactly when you're ready to move to the next level—and He will never take you there before it's time. He knows that premature promotion would only cause you to feel overwhelmed and behind. He's taking you by the hand and walking you through this, step by step. All you have to do is trust his timing.

Chapter Twelve

Shame

I've always been what some people might refer to as a "goody two shoes." I currently am and always have been a rule-follower. I didn't color outside of the lines in any way, shape or form, So you wouldn't think that shame would be something I struggled with if I had never really done anything drastically sinful to be ashamed of. I'm not saying I never made mistakes, I just didn't have the kind of past that made me look back and cringe about the way I had lived my life. But that's the thing about shame. It's different from guilt. It's different than feeling bad for your actions. Shame is much more sinister. Because if the enemy can't remind you of your mistakes, he'll try to convince you that you are one.

I'll be honest with you, this is the biggest and ugliest monster I have faced. And it still tries to rear its ugly head from time to time. I'm sure you've already seen it laced throughout some of my other stories. Shame attached itself to me from a very young age and could not be easily shaken. If you've ever dealt with shame in your life, I'm sure you know exactly what I'm talking about.

You already know what it's like to wonder if you belong anywhere and if the world would be better off without you. You're already familiar with the crushing assumption that you're a burden and a liability in every single room you step into. But that's not the truth of who you are. You're not a mistake, you are a masterpiece. If the God of the universe created you and was pleased with what He saw, what makes you think He could be wrong?

Shame has been lying to you, friend. Incessantly. It's been lying to you so much that you can't tell the difference between its whispers and the truth. But it doesn't have to have a hold on you anymore. With God's help, I was able to slay this dragon in my own life, so I know you can too. All it's going to take is latching onto the truth.

Not Enough

Ever since I was little, I've had the uncanny ability to see the best in people. Give me five minutes with someone and I guarantee you I can find something that I admire about them. It's almost like I can clearly see the potential and envision the future that could lie ahead of them if they would just lean into those gifts. If they would just lean into the truth of their identity. That doesn't sound like a bad skill to have, does it? It's really not. I love being able to see people the way that I imagine God sees them. It's absolutely beautiful. The only downside is when I start to internalize those things. When I'm around someone who is incredibly funny and start to realize how unfunny I am as a result.

Or when I see someone who is extremely talented and start to compare how my own talents measure up, or don't.

Shame started seeping in when I reached the point where I started to feel like I was underwhelming to everyone who met me. Unimpressive. Like I was only good enough until someone more interesting came along. Growing up, I was always Chuck and Pam's daughter. Elliott and Jesse's sister. The friend of the prettiest girl or the smartest guy. I never got to be just Caitlin. Because being just Caitlin didn't seem like it held enough weight. Everywhere I turned, it seemed like I was being overlooked or passed over for someone who had a better resume. I was picked last for every sport and every activity. Never chosen. And for a long time, that defined me. I practically had the word *unworthy* stamped on my forehead because that was what I truly believed about myself. That's such a defeating place to live, feeling like you're not worthy of being chosen by anyone.

I continued to feel that way for the majority of my life, until I got into a real relationship with God. See, I had been a Christian since I was eight years old. But I stayed in that caterpillar stage until I hit rock bottom in 2020. That was when the transformation began to take place. Turns out, rock bottom has a funny way of leading you to The Rock at the bottom. Once I truly turned to God during the hardest season of my life, He began to teach me new things about myself. While reading His Word, my eyes were opened to a new understanding of how much he valued me, as an individual. He wasn't passing me by. He wasn't overlooking me in search of someone more impressive. He saw me, flaws and all, and said, "I want this one."

Even though I finally felt seen, shame was still deeply embedded in me. I felt as though I had nothing of value to offer God. Come to find out, he actually likes it that way. Because when we feel like we have nothing to offer, that's when he is able to make up for the difference. The more deficient we are, the more easily we're able to recognize how powerful he is. This taught me to understand what Paul meant in 2 Corinthians 12:9. "But he said to me, 'My grace is sufficient for you, for my power is made perfect in weakness.' Therefore I will boast all the more gladly about my weaknesses, so that Christ's power may rest on me."

I was able to experience this first hand when God asked me to join TikTok and share what I was learning. For a solid week, I had to fight through the shame of feeling like I didn't have enough value to offer. I didn't have the proper lighting or the best camera. In those first videos I posted, I was sitting in my car stumbling over my words and praying that I was getting the right message across. I felt weak. Deficient. Ill-equipped. And yet, that was exactly where God's power came through. My first videos started to gain traction quickly. People were flooding to my page, waiting to hear more. And do you know what those people complimented me on the most? They told me how relatable I was. How much they could resonate with my message because I seemed like such a normal, ordinary person. Because I was one of them. God used the very thing that I thought disqualified me to spread the good news to thousands and thousands of people. His power was made perfect in my weakness.

The way I see it, we can live our lives one of two ways. We can either try to do everything ourselves, or we can surrender to what God wants to do with us by His side. Spoiler alert: God's way is always better. And when we lean into that, we get to fully relax into His love knowing that we are fully secure. Ephesians 1:4 says, "For he chose us in him before the creation of the world to be holy and blameless in his sight." Our value is not based on our performance, it's based on who God says we are. And He calls us chosen.

Several months ago, the looming threat of a TikTok ban was hanging in the air. At that point, my page had amassed nearly 140,000 followers. People that I knew personally would ask me if I was worried about the ban. "What are you going to do if TikTok goes away?" they would ask. "I feel bad for you, you worked so hard on it." Honestly, I wasn't worried. I didn't lose a minute of sleep over it because, deep down, I already knew the reality–I wasn't the one who made it successful. The success of that platform had nothing to do with my efforts. It was all God. If I had spent years striving for success and *trying* to gain those followers, then yes, losing all of that effort would've been a bummer. But there was zero striving involved. God chose to give me that assignment and He blessed it. If TikTok disappeared, He could just as easily give me a new assignment, or no assignment at all. At that point, I understood how valuable I was to my Father. I knew that if I did nothing but sit on my couch for the rest of my life, He would love me no less. And that was what brought me peace.

If you want freedom from the shame you feel, it's as simple as recognizing how precious you are to your Heavenly Father. He doesn't need you to perform in order to gain his attention. He doesn't need you to prove yourself. Psalms 147:11 says, "The Lord delights in those who fear him, who put their hope in his unfailing love." Did you catch that? Put your hope in His unfailing love. That is the only expectation He has of you, to trust how much He loves you. Leave the rest in His hands, and watch what He can do with it.

Too Much

Maybe shame hasn't told you that you're not good enough. Maybe that door has flung the opposite way and told you that you're too much. Or, if you're anything like me, maybe it told you that you were both at the same time. Deficient in certain areas, overcompensating in others. We all have parts of ourselves that come naturally to us that others seem to want to shave down. I can almost guarantee that every single person at one point or another has been told that there are parts of themselves that they need to tone down. So we whittle away at these parts of ourselves, trying to squeeze ourselves into the mold that others have told us we belong in. And when we inevitably fail, we feel shame for not being able to conform correctly.

The bottom line is that God did not create you to conform. Every piece of you that has been there since you were formed in your mother's womb is a necessary part of the puzzle. Sometimes, we just have to learn how to use them properly. If you've been in Christian circles for any length of time, I'm sure you've heard the term "meek" thrown around a time or two. Oftentimes, people equate meekness with being gentle, kind, or even timid. In Matthew 5:5, Jesus says, "Blessed are the meek, for they will inherit the earth." So frequently, we think this means that we have to become something we're not. That we have to remove any parts of ourselves that are not gentle and timid. What's interesting is that the original Greek word for meekness literally translates to "strength under control."

I recently learned that the term "meek" was originally used to describe war horses.[1] In those times, warriors would find packs of wild horses that had so much raw strength and power. They would then "meeken" those horses, meaning that they would tame them, bring them into submission, and channel that strength to be used in war. Here's what I want you to see. The characteristics of those horses were never removed, they were simply channeled in the right direction. They still retained every ounce of their power, strength, and strong will. The only difference is that under that submission, their power became an incredible weapon against the enemy.

---

1. Marg Mowczko, Meekness Is Not Weakness: Praus in the Bible (2018).

When I was sixteen, my parents gifted me with my first car. The first thing I wanted to do was put the key into the ignition and whip out of that driveway. There was so much freedom attached to having my own car and I was ready to taste it. My dad, however, had other plans. Before he would ever let me put the car in drive, he spent far too much time explaining to me what each of the buttons did and how they were to be used. I wanted to use my gift the way I wanted to use it, but he wanted me to use it the way it was intended to be used.

God seems to work in the same way. He's given us all of these extraordinary gifts that are so incredibly unique to each of us, but most of us rip through life without ever learning how to use them properly. If we can spend enough time with God to learn how He intended for us to use the strengths He gave us, we will see that all of the things we've been told are "too much" have been there for a reason all along.

Let me give you an example. I was always told that I was too sensitive. I've always had big emotions and I feel things very deeply. When I'm happy, I'm ecstatic. When I'm sad, that pain ripples through my system for days. Turns out, emotions can be kind of contagious. And when you're sad, some people seem to avoid you as if you literally have the plague. Throughout most of my life, the things that seemed like a big deal to me didn't seem to matter as much to other people. They would tell me that I needed to "get over it" and "not take things so seriously." But no matter how hard I tried, I never could seem to stuff those emotions down for long. Inevitably, they would come bubbling back up to the surface, which led to those familiar feelings of shame. *Why can't I keep a tight lid on my emotions like everyone else? What is wrong with me?* Little did I know that the very thing everyone else thought was wrong with me was the very thing God knew was right with me. He had a plan for all of it, I just didn't see it at the time.

See, I've always kind of been the friend that people come to for advice. People seem to love to talk to me about their problems. I don't necessarily think it's because I have anything groundbreaking to say, but more so because I'm a good listener. Any time my friends would come to me, they would tell me that they admired my ability to make them feel heard. Do you want to know why I'm able to make them feel heard? It's *because* I'm extra sensitive. How am I supposed to help people through things if I'm not sensitive enough to see that they're struggling in the first place? How am I supposed to make them feel understood and valued if I'm not at all familiar with the emotions they are expressing? That sensitivity was never a character flaw, it was a weapon. I just had to learn how to use it as such.

I don't know what it is that you've been told. Maybe people have told you that you're too loud. Or could it be possible that you're just loud enough to speak up for those who don't have a voice? Maybe you've been told that you're overly dramatic. But what if you're just dramatic enough to make people feel celebrated? Whatever that statement is for you, I can tell you this. That character trait wasn't put there by accident. It's not something you need to remove from your personality in order for God to love you or approve of you. It's simply something that needs to be meekened in order for it to be used as the weapon God intended it to be.

Victory over Shame

The revelation I'm about to share with you is something I can't take credit for. It came from a conversation I was a part of recently, and it's stuck with me ever since. Do you remember that verse that talks about us being new creations? It's 2 Corinthians 5:17. Here's what it says: "Therefore, if anyone is in Christ, the new creation has come: The old has gone, the new is here!" During this conversation, these women were sharing with me about how they always thought the word "gone" meant that it was in the past. Not that it ceased to exist, but that it just became something you've moved on from. But as they dug a little deeper into their word study, they realized that "gone" actually meant "dead." Deceased. No longer living. That was when one of the women shared one of the most profound revelations I've ever heard. She said, "I think all this time, I've been carrying a dead body around."

Did that hit you square in the chest like it did me? Man, that is powerful. So many times, we think that we're just supposed to be struck with this new identity, new mindsets, new habits. But the reality is, we have to make the choice to bury that old body. Shame will try to convince you to cling to the things of your past. It will try to tell you that who you always have been is who you always will be. Simultaneously too much and not enough. Listen to me, friend. Imagine me holding your hands and looking straight into your eyes as I say this. I need you to let these words land. That is not who you are anymore. It's time to bury your past. It's time to hold a funeral for the person you used to be. Because carrying that dead weight around is doing nothing but holding you back.

On the other hand, let me also say this. It's okay to grieve for the person that you once were. It's okay to mourn for that child that no one protected, for that teen that felt like the world was against them, for that young adult that felt like they had no one in their corner. You are not doing them a disservice by burying them where they lie. You are honoring their memory by stepping into who you were always created to be. I won't lie to you, it can be scary to become a person that you feel like you don't know. It's a strange experience to look in the mirror and feel like you don't recognize the person that you're becoming. But that doesn't mean that they're not worth getting to know. Don't allow shame to have a grip on your life anymore. Don't allow it to weigh you down. Bury the old, step into the new, and I think you'll find the person you've been looking for all along.

Chapter Thirteen

Fight Back

I've told you from the very beginning of this book that this path to victory wouldn't be easy. But the cold, hard truth is that it's not just difficult, it can be downright brutal. The upside is that there is always something rewarding on the other side of every single battle you fight. As my pastor likes to say, when the hard times come, you can become the victim or the victor. You can get bitter, or you can get better.

I'm not a die-hard sports fan by any stretch of the imagination. However, I do occasionally enjoy watching professional football. For the longest time, I didn't understand the rules of the game until I married someone who finally took the time to explain it to me. I just remember watching those games and thinking about how interesting it was that if you didn't have the ball, you were practically invisible. But as soon as you got that ball in your possession, every single one of those grown men on that field would treat you as if you had just abducted their first born child. They became absolutely ravenous. Why? Because their sole mission was to keep that person from moving further down the field.

When you start abandoning these old mindsets that have been holding you back for so long, you will inevitably start to move the ball down the field. And you're delusional if you think that the devil is just going to sit back and watch you do it. In fact, when you start to make progress, he's going to throw everything he possibly can at you to try and make you fumble. It's the nature of the game. But try as he might, he cannot win.

I've seen a few nasty football games in my day, but there was one game in particular that was especially excruciating to watch. One team was getting absolutely clobbered by the other. The scoreboard was reflecting an absolute annihilation of the losing team. And yet, the losing team kept fighting. These guys were scrappy. It was clear they were not going down without a fight. I remember thinking *Why don't they just give up? There's not enough time left on the clock. They're clearly never going to win.* At that point, it was explained to me that even though the losing team would never have enough time to score enough points to have a victory, their pride was at stake. The bigger the deficit on the scoreboard, the more their ego was bruised. They weren't fighting for a victory, they were fighting for their pride. They were fighting to keep themselves from being too embarrassed by everyone watching. Because if they gave up now, the loss would be absolutely tragic.

Let me make this abundantly clear. The enemy cannot defeat you. He's already lost. The time on the clock may not be up yet, but the scoreboard is reflecting that it's as good as done. The worst he can do to you is try and keep you from moving forward. He will try to do everything in his power to knock you down, even if it's only for a few seconds. Even if he knows you will get back up again. That's the only move he's got. And it's not so that he can beat you, it's so that you can't beat him worse than you already are.

This is the mental battle that we have to face each and every day. Are we going to continue feeling defeated, refusing to get back up, just waiting for the time to run down until the final whistle is blown? Because that is an option. You are not required to keep fighting. You can absolutely choose to stay exactly where you are and you will be loved no less because of it. But if you make that choice, you're robbed of the joy that comes from participating in a victory. If you refuse to fight, you don't get the satisfaction of looking up at the final scoreboard and saying *Wow, I played a part in that.*

I know that sometimes we lack the motivation to move forward. Sometimes the blows we take knock the wind right out of us and we struggle to see the benefit in rising to our feet. The enemy would love nothing more than to convince your imagination that he's actually doing something detrimental. And, while I know that the circumstances in our lives can feel dire at times, that doesn't mean we've been defeated. Jesus already went to the cross. Those of us who have accepted Jesus' sacrifice have already been adopted into the King's family. We're already on the winning team. There is nothing the enemy can do to take that away from you and he knows it. Your only job now is to keep going. Keep pushing. Keep fighting. Not because we need it to win, but because the further we go, the more we reflect the restorative power of our Father to those around us, and to the generations to come.

Armor Up

Every family has one of those stories that they love to tell over and over again because it just never gets old. In my family, one of those stories is about the time that the woods behind our house caught fire. I grew up in a home that was surrounded by trees. In order to keep our yard well-maintained, my dad would collect any limbs or sticks that had fallen from those trees, pile them up and start a bonfire. Not only did this help minimize the amount of limbs in our yard, but this also gave us plenty of excuses to roast marshmallows.

On this particular occasion, however, my dad had not done the best job at making sure the fire was properly extinguished after all of the limbs were burned. That night, he went to bed while the leftover embers got to work. Early the next morning, we were woken up by the sound of the phone ringing. It was my neighbor, calling my parents to inform them that there was a blazing inferno in the woods behind our house. My dad and brother rushed out of the house barely even taking the time to put shoes on. My brother, naturally, snatched up the water hose and turned it on full blast. Smart move. My dad, on the other hand, grabbed a shovel. *A shovel.* How was he supposed to put out a miniature forest fire with a shovel? He defended his choice by saying that if a shovel was good enough for Smokey the Bear, it was good enough for him.

As funny as this story is to reflect on, I think if most of us were honest with ourselves, we could admit that we kind of do the same thing. We have an entire army of hell that is out to stop us in whatever way they can. And yet, most of us are showing up to fight that fire with a shovel. Maybe we don't take it seriously. Maybe we think that our actions are of little consequence. Maybe we expect God to fight all of our battles for us. Regardless of what excuse we have, the Bible tells us that we have to be vigilant against these attacks.

Ephesians 6:14-17 says, "Stand firm then, with the belt of truth buckled around your waist, with the breastplate of righteousness in place, and with your feet fitted with the readiness that comes from the gospel of peace. In addition to all this, take up the shield of faith, with which you can extinguish all the flaming arrows of the evil one. Take the helmet of salvation and the sword of the Spirit, which is the word of God." The truth is, I can talk until I'm blue in the face, telling you about all of the mindset shifts you can make and all of the tactics you can try to overcome the enemy, but no amount of advice I can give you will ever be stronger than the Word of God. If we are not choosing to read our Bibles and actually apply it to our lives, we are showing up to the battle ill-equipped, just like my dad was that day.

James 1:22-25 says, "Do not merely listen to the word, and so deceive yourselves. Do what it says. Anyone who listens to the word but does not do what it says is like someone who looks at his face in a mirror and, after looking at himself, goes away and immediately forgets what he looks like. But whoever looks intently into the perfect law that gives freedom, and continues in it—not forgetting what they have heard, but doing it—they will be blessed in what they do." Did you catch the promise in the last part of that passage? If we actually put the Word of God into practice in our lives, we will be blessed in what we do. I don't know about you, but that sounds an awful lot like victory to me. Does that mean that everything will work out in our favor? Not always. But it does mean that God will work it all together for our ultimate good.

I know, sometimes that can sound a whole lot like one of those Christian sayings that everyone says, but no one really understands. What does it even mean to apply the Word of God to your life? How do you even do that? Well, you see, the Bible is not just a love letter from our Father to us. It's also an instruction manual. We're told story after story about how God shows up in the lives of His people. And we're given story after story about how humans either leaned in or ran away, along with the consequences of each. So what do we do with that information? How do we use it to improve our own walk with God?

When my brother was in high school, he played for the varsity basketball team. And maybe I'm just biased because I'm his sister, but from my perspective, he was ridiculously good at it. It was incredible to watch that team work like a well-oiled machine. Some players were so in sync with each other that they could complete passes without even looking. Do you want to know why they were so good? One of the reasons was because they would watch film. The coach had a rotation of people that would use a video camera to record the entire game. I happened to be one of the people that was tasked with capturing each and every second of play. During practice that week, they would take time to watch those tapes and dissect what went wrong and what went right. They even studied the opposing team's strategies in order to learn how to adjust so that they could more easily defeat them next time. They would decide what areas they needed to strengthen and improve on. And here's the kicker. They would then go and apply the lessons that they learned to their practice sessions. If the team seemed to be missing their free throws, they would practice free throws. If the team was getting overly exhausted in the fourth quarter, they would do conditioning drills. Whatever areas needed to be worked on were worked out in those practices. And because of their dedication, their team only improved as they went along.

I want you to think about the stories in your Bible like film to be studied. Run it back, time and time again. Study what went wrong, and study what went right. Identify the areas where you need the most improvement and then go practice it until you get better. Apply it to your life. Use it as a tool to get you closer to where you need to be. If your biggest struggle is insecurity, study the story of what happened when Sarah was so insecure about not being able to give Abraham a child that she had him sleep with Hagar instead. Take a good look at how that story played out in the years to come. Then you could look at Queen Esther, who seemed to struggle with imposter syndrome, feeling as though she had no authority in the kingdom she was ruling over. You could study how she overcame that insecurity and trusted God to use her actions for good. Ask the Holy Spirit to show you how to use that information to create strategies that will help you overcome the insecurities in your own life. Then take those strategies and put them into practice.

Maybe your biggest struggle is fear. Study all of the stories in the Bible where people had an opportunity to be afraid. There are *plenty* of them. What happened to those who let fear take over? What happened to those who felt the fear and did it anyway? How can you apply those lessons to your own life so that you can overcome that fear? Whether you relate to any of the struggles that we've discussed in this book, or you have a few more of your own, I can promise you that the Bible has a strategy to help you overcome it. God didn't leave anything out or overlook any issue when He knit those narratives together. All you have to do is study it, apply it, and armor up to join the fight.

Rest is a Battle Strategy

One other thing I want you to notice about the armor of God is that there is nothing to cover your back. That's because we are not meant to retreat. We are not meant to back down. We are meant to armor up, to press forward, and to refuse to stop until the battle is won. But where does rest fit into this? Are we really meant to keep spinning our wheels until we can't possibly keep going? Of course not. So let's talk about how to incorporate rest, not as a result of exhaustion, but as a tool to help you keep fighting.

When I was younger, my mom used to run marathons with her best friend. They would wake up before dawn and run several miles multiple times a week. They would train and train and train some more until their bodies were physically prepared for everything they were about to demand of them. The interesting thing about the training process is that a couple of weeks before they were set to run their longest distance, they would rest. In those few weeks, they would gradually reduce the number of miles they were running until they whittled it down to just a brisk jog, with rest days in between. Isn't that strange? I mean, it's not like they were tired. They had just spent all that time preparing their bodies to handle extreme distances. They weren't resting from a place of fatigue, they were resting from a place of preparation.

We all seem to have this natural instinct to want to keep pushing forward until we're tired. I'm convinced it's human nature. Just ask any toddler who is being forced to take a nap. The first thing out of their mouths will be "But I not tired!" At least, that's what my kids would always say. They didn't like to rest when they felt like they had more energy to burn off. The truth is, we don't always like when God asks us to rest either. He always seems to ask us to rest when we feel as though we can keep going. We think of it more as an inconvenience. We insist that we are not tired. That we can keep pushing forward. That we will be sure to rest once we reach the point of exhaustion. But if all we do is rest when we are exhausted, we're completely missing the point.

After the Israelites had exited Egypt and entered the wilderness, they were trying to unlearn the old ways of the Egyptians and relearn the ways of God. During this time, God instructs them to rest on the seventh day of each week. This is what Exodus 16:23 says, "He said to them, 'This is what the Lord commanded: 'Tomorrow is to be a day of sabbath rest, a holy sabbath to the Lord. So bake what you want to bake and boil what you want to boil. Save whatever is left and keep it until morning.'" Now, why would He tell them to do this? They had just come from a place where they worked all day every day. They were used to being productive. Used to being busy. And now, all of a sudden, God is wanting them to just sit around every day? All they have to do is collect the food and water He provides and worship Him? But who was going to construct the buildings? Who was going to reestablish the economy and make trades with other nations and conquer territories? You see, the Israelites were making the same mistake that most of us make today. When we are constantly productive, constantly busy, never taking time to rest, we fall into the trap of thinking that any blessing that comes as a result of that was put there by our own hand, and not by God's. Strategically resting helps us to remember who we are and who we belong to. It also helps us position ourselves for battle.

Think about it this way. When you only make time for rest after you're exhausted, what are you going to do when the enemy uses that moment to attack? You'll do nothing. Because you'll be too exhausted. You won't have the strength or the energy to fight back. However, if you were to strategically take the time to rest before you ever feel tired, whenever the enemy comes to attack, you will be ready for him, because your energy was never depleted in the first place. You can never prepare if you're always pushing. Just like my mom's strategic rest prepared her body for the marathon ahead, your strategic rest will prepare you for whatever lies ahead of you.

Embrace the Process

Here's what I don't want to happen. I don't want you to read this book and think that these battles are "one and done." It takes more than one battle to win a war, and it's going to take more than one battle for you to conquer these false mindsets. You'll overcome one fear and feel like you're on top of the world, and then a larger fear will rear its ugly head. You'll slay one insecurity, and a few months later, an even bigger insecurity will come busting down your door. This is a lifelong battle of sanctification. But on the other side of each of these battles is a little more freedom than you had before.

Listen, I am not in any way trying to sell you the idea that if you're spiritual enough, you won't struggle with these things any longer. You're human. Of course you will. What I do want you to see is that *as* you wrestle with these things, you can find more and more freedom along the way. The truth is, I still struggle with each and every one of the things I mentioned earlier. In fact, a lot of these struggles came back to bite me as I was writing this book.

Insecurity tried to tell me that if people read about the things I've struggled with, they would reject me. Pride tried to convince me that I needed to protect my reputation. People pleasing told me I should be concerned about what people would say about some of the stories I chose to include. Victimhood tried to tell me that there was nothing I could do about those tormenting thoughts. Negativity told me my book wasn't any good. Fear told me that everyone that read it would view me differently. Loneliness told me that because I was the only one facing this battle, I had no support. And shame tried to convince me that everything I do is a mistake. They were all wrong, but they were all very loud.

I've done a lot of coaching in this book. And I don't ever want you to think that I'm unwilling to lead by example. The fact that you are reading these words is proof that I conquered all of those thoughts that were screaming at me that this book was a bad idea. I felt the fear, and I did it anyway. So as you flip through these final pages, let this be a physical reminder to you that you can do this too. Those thoughts do not have to have a hold on you any longer. You are not a slave to that way of thinking anymore. You are no longer required to live in defeat. It's time to step into your victory.

Chapter Fourteen

Victory

Remember at the beginning of this book when I said that at some point you would probably want to shut it and not open it ever again? Well, congratulations! If you're reading this, that means you stuck it out to the very end. I'm so proud of you. You're not the type to shy away from the hard stuff or back down from a fight. Because that's just what this is–a fight. The word victory itself implies that there is a battle to be won. Victory is not something that happens by accident. It's not something that just falls into your lap. It is a fight that must be faced and conquered.

If I asked you to define what victory looks like, what would you say? I think most people have a tendency to think that victory in your life will mean a change in your circumstances. In a way, we sometimes equate victory with success. If we are successful in business, we define that success by the amount of money we make. If we are successful in our careers, we define it by the status or position we hold. But what if victory meant something else entirely? What if victory wasn't defined by your circumstances, but by how you react despite them?

You see, we don't measure our victories by our ability to change our circumstances. In order to be victorious, we have to remember who our adversary is. We're not fighting against our circumstances, we're fighting against the enemy. Our circumstances are just the sword he uses to try and cut us down. So how do we defeat him even if our circumstances never change? We have to let him know that no matter what situations he may throw at us, we will not quit. You cannot defeat someone who refuses to stay down.

Fight from Victory, Not for Victory

Be honest. When it comes to this battle you've been given to fight, you've probably, at some point, felt like you've been dealt a losing hand. Am I right? That's why you've felt defeated in the first place. It seems like a battle you can't possibly win, so you've struggled to even find the motivation to try.

Do you remember the movie *Speed*? It was a 1994 film starring Sandra Bullock and Keaneu Reeves. In this movie, they unknowingly board a bus that's been strapped with a bomb. This bomb is set to go off if the bus reaches a speed that is below 50 miles per hour. As expected, this presents a lot of complications as they struggle to try and help people get off of the bus safely while navigating road work, traffic, and other obstacles that threaten to blow them to smithereens. Sometimes, I think that's how we approach spiritual warfare. We tend to live in this high-stress, life or death state of mind, thinking that if we make one wrong move, it's game over.

What if I told you that it's possible to fight *from* a place of victory and not *for* the victory? I know, I know. You've probably heard this a million times. But nobody ever seems to be able to explain what that phrase means or how to accomplish that task, do they? It's a hard concept to understand. If we've already won, why does fighting sometimes feel like the hardest thing we will ever do? If the victory is already ours, why does it feel so fragile? Let me set your mind at ease. Because what I want you to see is that you haven't been dealt a losing hand at all. You've actually been dealt the best possible hand, you just have to be taught how to play your cards right.

I want you to think about your battle more as a sword fight. I feel like I should put a disclaimer here. I've never actually participated in a sword fight. But I have picked up a few tidbits of knowledge here and there from watching combat movies and Olympic fencing. One of the things I've learned is that when it comes to sword fighting, the one who is advancing is the one who has the upper hand in the match. If you can back your opponent into a corner, the match is as good as done. The truth is, when you are the one being forced to retreat, the best you can do is try and defend yourself from every blow the opponent sends your way. But if you can be the one to make your enemy retreat, their defeat is inevitable. They may keep swinging. They may keep trying to slice at you and cut you deeply, but so long as you hold your position, they cannot gain the upper hand. Their defeat is inevitable. So let me ask you this. Which one of those opponents do you want to be? The one retreating? Or the one advancing?

You see, when Jesus rose from the grave, He gave us the upper hand over everything we would ever face in this life. He conquered death, hell, and everything in it once and for all. He gave you the power to advance against your enemy. We were no longer doomed to be forced to retreat. The problem is that most of us just don't know that. Or if we do know that we have authority, we just aren't sure how to use it.

Allow me to give you an actual example of how this works. There is a Christian music artist named Forrest Frank who recently broke his back while skateboarding in his driveway. His feet slipped out from under him and he landed spine first on the curb of the concrete. Ouch. To us, that may look like the enemy had really done some damage right? Forrest was seriously injured. He was wounded in battle. According to his circumstances, it looked as though the enemy had the upper hand. But then something interesting happened. As Forrest was lying on his bed in excruciating pain, he began to record songs about how God had his back (pun intended) and about how Jesus can turn lemons into lemonade. Shortly after he released those songs, they began to climb to the top of the charts. Then, two weeks after his initial injury, he was miraculously healed. He was able to get out of bed and walk around with no pain. He even went and got an x-ray that proved that the fractures in his back had completely disappeared within 14 days of their occurrence. As a result of this, Forrest's career exploded. His music began to surpass artists not only on the

Christian charts, but in secular realms, too. His work was already well-known, but after that incident, he was well on his way to becoming a household name.

Now, let me ask you this. What do you think was his point of victory here? Was it when his new music started to climb the charts like never before? Was it when his back was miraculously healed? Or was it when his name was in the mouths of people who had never heard of him before and his notoriety began to spread around the globe? What if I told you that none of those things were what marked Forrest's victory? We tend to think that victory equals a change in our circumstances. So whenever Forrest's circumstances began to change, that was when he became victorious, right? I disagree.

To me, the moment that Forrest became victorious was the moment that he opened his mouth to sing, despite what was happening around him. That was when he chose to send a message to the enemy that he was not going to retreat. He was not going to wallow in self-pity. He was not going to feel sorry for himself. He was going to advance and make hell pay for the damages. That moment that he chose to praise God and give God glory in the midst of a broken situation was what caused the enemy to back up. And when the enemy backed up, God had room to work. Everything that came afterwards was a result of God's hand. All Forrest did was make a conscious decision to partner with God, no matter what the outcome.

The truth is that our circumstances don't always change. Sometimes things get worse before they get better. But when we refuse to cower to our adversary's intimidation tactics, it shows God that we trust Him. It is a conscious effort to put our faith in Him. And faith is the catalyst that can cause a change in our circumstances as God begins to work everything for our good, whether we recognize it right away or much further down the road.

Faithful to the End

The apostle Paul describes our Christian walk as a race that we are running. (1 Corinthians 9:24). Remember when I told you about my mom running marathons? As thrilling as it sounds to get out there and complete a marathon, nobody gets to that point quickly. It takes time and dedication. So if our entire lives are one big marathon of faith, as Paul suggests, that means it's going to require time and dedication to experience that victory. We have to practice trusting God. And the more we practice throughout our day, the more trust is developed along the way.

The extent to which you are willing to trust God is the extent to which you will experience freedom in your life. The apostle Paul seemed to understand this concept better than most. I know I mentioned this story earlier in the book, but I think it's worth taking another look. Allow me to set the scene. Paul and Silas had just been preaching the gospel when a woman who was heavily involved in witchcraft started taunting them (Acts 16). Finally, Paul had had enough of it, so he called the unclean spirit to come out of her. The problem was that fortune telling was a very lucrative business, and her bosses were not happy that they had just lost their cash cow. So they dragged Paul and Silas into the public square to be severely beaten and arrested. And as if that weren't enough, they weren't just thrown into jail, but locked in an inner cell with their feet in stocks so that they couldn't even walk around.

I don't know about you, but I would imagine that if I were in their shoes, I would probably be tempted to complain about how unfair that sequence of events was. They were just out preaching the gospel, seeing others be healed, delivered, and set free and this was the thanks they got? Being brutally beaten, humiliated, and locked up like animals? Is this how God rewards His servants for their good and faithful works? What we neglect to notice is that this was all a part of a much bigger picture. Let's take a look at what happens next. This story comes from Acts 16:25-34.

> "About midnight Paul and Silas were praying and singing hymns to God, and the other prisoners were listening to them. Suddenly there was such a violent earthquake that the foundations of the prison were shaken. At once all the prison doors flew open, and everyone's chains came loose. The jailer woke up, and when he saw the prison doors open, he drew his sword and was about to kill himself because he thought the prisoners had escaped. But Paul shouted, 'Don't harm yourself! We are all here!' The jailer called for lights, rushed in and fell

> trembling before Paul and Silas. He then brought them out and asked, 'Sirs, what must I do to be saved?' They replied, 'Believe in the Lord Jesus, and you will be saved—you and your household.' Then they spoke the word of the Lord to him and to all the others in his house. At that hour of the night the jailer took them and washed their wounds; then immediately he and all his household were baptized. The jailer brought them into his house and set a meal before them; he was filled with joy because he had come to believe in God—he and his whole household."

You've probably heard this story before. And when you did hear it, I'm sure your focus was the fact that they were miraculously freed from prison. That's the moment of victory, right? That's the reason they were praying and singing, because they knew that if they had the right attitude, God would rescue them...right? A few years ago, that was what I thought. I thought that an attitude of gratitude was the magic button that you needed to push if you wanted to receive a miracle. However, after going through all of the things I've been through over the past five years, I tend to view this story a little differently these days.

What I noticed is that even when they got their miracle, they didn't take it right away. Instead, they stayed in their cells. They chose to sit in those uncomfortable circumstances for longer than necessary. Why? For the sake of the gospel. For the sake of the guard's salvation, and the salvation of his entire household. For the sake of the bigger picture. They weren't merely concerned about getting out of prison so they could continue on their merry way. They were concerned about the souls of every single person in their vicinity. They were so focused on the mission that the circumstances didn't matter. They understood that God could use any circumstance–yes, even imprisonment—to allow them to play a part in furthering His kingdom. And rather than being rewarded with a comfortable life, they were rewarded with the hope of salvation. They received an eternal reward for bringing someone into God's family. And that kind of reward will never, ever expire.

How do you think Paul came to this conclusion in the first place? How did he know beyond a shadow of a doubt that God could use *anything*, even death itself, to further His mission to rescue His people? My theory is that Paul saw this first hand before his conversion ever happened. You see, before Paul became Paul, he was a religious leader named Saul who was known for persecuting and even killing Christians. There's one in particular that I'm sure he never forgot. During Saul's crusade to try and rid his region of Christianity, he bumped into a man named Stephen who just would not shut up about the love of Jesus. One day, the religious leaders had had enough of it. They decided that they were going to shut him up once and for all by stoning him to death.

Stephen is the first recorded martyr in the history of Christianity. But it's not just the fact that he was willing to die for his faith that's impressive. Even more impactful than that is how he died, and the results that followed. Acts 7:59-60 says, “While they were stoning him, Stephen prayed, ‘Lord Jesus, receive my spirit.’ Then he fell on his knees and cried out, ‘Lord, do not hold this sin against them.’ When he had said this, he fell asleep.” Even though Stephen was faithful right up to the end, his circumstances didn’t change. He still died. But he received a far greater reward than escaping with his life. The latter half of Revelation 2:10 says, “Be faithful, even to the point of death, and I will give you life as your victor’s crown.” He may not have been given an extended life here on earth, but he received the eternal reward of the crown of life. And if you were able to ask him, I’m sure he would say it was worth it. Because that wasn’t the only result of his stoning.

Right after Stephen’s death, Acts 8:1-2 says, “And Saul approved of their killing him. On that day a great persecution broke out against the church in Jerusalem, and all except the apostles were scattered throughout Judea and Samaria.” Did you catch that? Stephen’s death meant that the rest of the Christians scattered throughout Judea and Samaria. Which meant that while Saul was trying to kill off one Christian, he accidentally contributed to a whole movement of Christianity breaking out across the nation.

When you live in the country like I do, you tend to encounter a lot of bugs on a daily basis. It’s not unusual to see spiders all around the farm and throughout the woods. Normally, if I see a spider I will leave it alone, unless it’s infiltrated an area where it shouldn’t be. Like inside my house. I can coexist with insects on my property, but I draw the line when they try to become my roommate without my consent. I can remember one time when a giant spider made it's way into my living room. Naturally, I grabbed a flip flop to rid myself of the problem. Except, when I lifted my shoe after delivering a satisfying blow, I was even more horrified. The spider was carrying an egg sack. By killing the mother, I had just released hundreds of baby spiders into my home. Instead of ridding myself of a problem, I had just created a bigger one. I'm sure Saul felt the same way after Stephen's death. Sure, he had rid himself of one Christian, but he had just released thousands of others. He got to see with His own eyes that God can use quite literally anything to work for the good of His people.

I'm sure this is what contributed to Paul eventually becoming so bold in his faith. He knew from firsthand experience that the enemy could not do anything to him that wouldn't backfire. Paul knew that even if he were to die for his faith, that God would use that for an eternal purpose. He trusted God not only with his circumstances, but with his life. And he absolutely refused to give in to the intimidation tactics of the enemy. When you think about it, that's really what victory boils down to. It's not a change in your circumstances, it's a stubborn refusal to let your adversary gain the upper hand.

When I was old enough to babysit my sister, I used to watch her in the summertime while my parents were at work. One summer, she wanted to do nothing but watch Mulan every single day. Sometimes twice a day. I can probably recite the entire movie by heart because of that one summer. But there's one line in particular that has stuck with me more than the others. Towards the end of the movie, it looks as though all hope is lost. The Huns–ruthless killers who do not even spare the lives of innocent children–have infiltrated the city. The leader of the Huns corners the unprotected emperor and draws his sword, demanding that the emperor bow to him. The emperor's response sends chills up my spine every time I hear it. He says, "No matter how the wind howls, the mountain cannot bow to it."

Doesn't that sound an awful lot like the situations we find ourselves in sometimes? It looks like all hope has been lost. It feels as though the enemy has us cornered on all sides, demanding that we bow to him. It seems like a matter of life or death. And yet, even in those dire situations, we still have a choice on whether or not we bend a knee. We can still refuse to give the enemy an inch of satisfaction that he has won. That no matter how much he howls, we cannot and *will not* bow. We can adopt the kind of boldness that allows us to look the enemy right in his face and tell him that we'd rather die on our feet than live on our knees. That we will no longer bend to his agenda, no matter what it costs us. Because we know, beyond a shadow of a doubt, that we serve a God who can and *will* use each and every situation we go through for our good. So we will use this situation that we are walking through as an opportunity to pledge our allegiance to the Alpha and Omega. The one who remains faithful even when we are faithless. The one who loves us through our difficulties, even when we can't see it. *That* is the side we choose, and nothing the devil can throw at us can make us change our minds.

Chapter Fifteen

The Bigger Picture

Have you ever heard the saying, "You can't see the forest for the trees"? It sounds kind of silly, doesn't it? Someone is complaining about not being able to see the forest because of all the trees that are in the way. But the trees *are* the forest. Much like that saying, a lot of us get so hung up on the small details of what's happening in our lives that we can't see how those details are all part of a larger story that's being told.

I recently started working on an idea for a fiction book, as if I don't have enough to do. What I quickly learned is that crafting a story is entirely different from writing non-fiction. Storytelling takes immense attention to detail. No good author is going to plug details into a storyline that don't make sense or that have nothing to do with the main plot. Every good author knows that absolutely nothing can be wasted. If you look at Hebrews 12:2, some translations (like NASB) refer to Jesus as "the author and perfecter of our faith." God is the best author there is. My guy knows how to tell a good story. So if you are allowing Him to write your life's story, that means that not a single detail of it is going to go to waste. All of it is being used for a bigger plot.

However, the big picture can be really difficult to see at times. We can listen to all of the pep talks and encouragement we want, but at the end of the day (because we're human), we're all still secretly wondering what's in it for us? What is the whole point of this if we're just meant to struggle through life until it's over? What do we gain by running this race with all of our might, changing our mindsets, and standing up to the enemy? I'm so glad you asked. See, I had a lot of those same questions. So let's break down what's in it for you, so that you can see how all of these sometimes unfortunate details are setting you up for the most beautiful story.

Victory Brings You Freedom

I've said it from the beginning. There is nothing easy about this walk. I hope I've made it very clear that if you want the victory, you've got to fight for it. Your anointing is going to cost you. The purer the oil, the heavier it is. But, be encouraged, because this journey is going to benefit you greatly.

Think about the story of Shadrach, Meshach and Abednego (found in Daniel 3). If anyone knows what it's like to fight a mental battle, it's them. Here they are, being commanded to bow down to a false idol that King Nebuchadnezzar created. And because they refuse, their very lives are at stake. Not only are they about to be executed, but they're about to be thrown into the fire. I don't know about you, but when I think about all of the ways I would want to go out, being thrown into a fire is towards the bottom of my list. Being in excruciating pain while my flesh is quite literally melting off of my bones does not sound like an even remotely pleasant way to go.

Listen, I'm of Irish descent. I can catch a nasty sunburn after just 20 minutes outside. I can also be pretty clumsy, which means I've burnt my hand on the stove more than a couple of times. I'm well acquainted with the effects of heat on the skin, so I am in no way trying to play with fire. If I were in the same position, I'm not sure I would have the gall to muster the same courage they did.

Yet here these men are, being faced with one of the worst ways to die, and they don't even seem to flinch. In fact, they openly admit that they *don't know* if God is going to save them or not. Look at what they say in Daniel 3:17-18 (emphasis added). "If we are thrown into the blazing furnace, the God we serve is able to deliver us from it, and he will deliver us from Your Majesty's hand. *But even if he does not*, we want you to know, Your Majesty, that we will not serve your gods or worship the image of gold you have set up."

I can't imagine being in their position. They're basically saying, "Go ahead and threaten us, King Neb. You don't scare us! God is going to save us...*we think?*" I don't know about you, but I've walked through some things in my life that have required some pretty great faith, but most of those times, I was beyond convinced that God *would* save me. I'm not trying to risk my life for a *maybe.* But that's just me. Maybe that's an area where I need to grow.

Regardless, the point is, they get thrown into the fire, but before that happens, they are bound with ropes.

Okay, don't miss this. Because this part is really cool. Do you remember what happens after they get thrown into the fire? Let's read it. This is from Daniel 3:21-25 (emphasis added).

> So these men, wearing their robes, trousers, turbans and other clothes, were bound and thrown into the blazing furnace. The king's command was so urgent and the furnace so hot that the flames of the fire killed the soldiers who took up Shadrach, Meshach and Abednego, and these three men, *firmly tied*, fell into the blazing furnace. Then King Nebuchadnezzar leaped to his feet in amazement and asked his advisers, "Weren't there three men that we tied up and threw into the fire?" They replied, "Certainly, Your Majesty." He said, "Look! I see four men walking around in the fire, *unbound and unharmed*, and the fourth looks like a son of the gods."

Did you catch it? These men fell into the fire, *firmly tied,* and then emerged out of the other side, *unbound and unharmed*. In fact, verse 27 says that they didn't even smell like smoke when they came out of the other side. Don't you see? Whatever fire you are being put through right now is not meant to harm you, it's meant to *free* you. But sometimes, in order to get to your freedom, you have to walk through the fire that removes what binds you.

Before my son was born, I was terrified of even the idea of motherhood. It wasn't that I didn't want children, I just didn't seem to have those natural maternal instincts that other women had. Growing up, I didn't obsess over baby dolls or playing house or imagining what my family would look like. Naturally, my husband was ready for kids far before I was. It took him a solid six months to convince me that I wouldn't be an abysmal failure as a parent. And so, we started trying for a family. Three months later, my son was on the way.

Once he was born, things looked a whole lot different than I expected. Somehow, I had gotten the idea in my head that having a baby meant you'd be constantly surrounded by people who can help you. Maybe it was the TV shows I'd watched or the pictures I'd seen on social media, but that was my expectation. And for the first few weeks, I did have plenty of help. But after that, once the newness wore off and everyone had to go back to work, I felt utterly alone. My closest family was at least 30 minutes away and everyone I knew to ask for help all had full time jobs. My husband went back to his demanding work schedule and I was all alone, for at least 10 hours a day. I was running on very little sleep with a child who would not stop screaming because he was hungry and I couldn't even seem to figure out how to feed him properly. All of my worst fears were coming true. *I'm failing him.* That was what I thought. Just as I had imagined, I was a failure of a mother, or so it seemed.

One night, my husband came home to find both of us crying. And I don't just mean silent, tired tears falling down my cheeks. My son and I were both on the living room floor, sobbing and screaming. My shirt was covered in spit up because whatever I did feed him, he was unable to keep down. He was hungry, I was tired, and neither of us could seem to find a way out of it. Not to sound dramatic, but it was one of those moments where I felt like I had been bound and thrown into an all-consuming fire. Except this fire was made of guilt and shame and fear. And lots of tears.

At that moment, my husband scooped my son up and made him a bottle. Once I had a minute to regain my composure, we had a nice long talk. "I don't think I can do this," I said. Now, let me clarify. I wasn't saying that I didn't think I could be a mother. I just didn't think I could be a mother *alone.* All my life, I have lacked self-confidence. Yes, my parents raised me to be independent, but I was only independent when I had to be. If there was someone more capable around, I would shrink back and let them handle things, only stepping up if no one else was there to do whatever needed to be done. I didn't ever trust myself. I thought of myself as the least capable person in any room I was in. And that mindset had kept me bound my entire life.

"Everyone else seems to have help," I continued. "Everyone else lives close to family, or has a grandmother that doubles as a built-in babysitter. I don't have any support. If I am absolutely at my wits end and I call someone to ask for help, it will be at least an hour before they can get here, and by that point I've already lost my mind. I don't know what to do." That was the moment that my husband took my face in his hands, looked me in the eyes and said, "You *can* do this. No, you don't have a lot of support, but that is going to make you stronger. It's going to make you a better mom. Our kids are going to have such a strong bond with you because they won't know anyone else as their caregiver." Something about that statement seemed to snap the ropes that had been keeping me tied up for decades. *This will make you a better mom. They won't know anyone else as their caregiver.*

Could my husband have helped me find another solution? Sure. Could he have cut back on his hours at work or hired someone to come help me a few times a week? Of course. But my husband was able to see what I couldn't in that moment. He was able to see the bigger picture. He knew that if he found help for me, it would've reinforced the mindset that I needed rescuing, which would've done more harm than good in the long run. Instead, he chose to lean into what God was trying to do in this situation. He chose to allow me to walk through this fire, because he knew I would come out the other side unbound and unharmed. And boy, did I.

As the years went on, I developed such a strong, unbreakable bond with my children. As a family, we had created such a solid foundation. My kids listened to me. Our family thrived in a way I never thought possible. And I attribute it to those initial years when I had to walk through that fire all by myself. These days, I'm able to take my kids everywhere I go without a second thought. I'm no longer frazzled by the idea of having to run errands while my children tag along. It felt natural, like a mama duck who always has her little ducklings in tow. Right up until the moment they started school, they were my little sidekicks and I wouldn't have had it any other way.

Now, I understand that this isn't the path for everyone. Not every mother has the ability to stay home with their children. Not every woman would've cracked under the pressure that I endured. The point is, you're going to have to walk through hard things. Maybe leaving your children to go back to work is the hard thing that God is having you walk through. Maybe you've been bound by the idea that being a mother is your only identity and he's trying to break that lie off of you by showing you that you have an individual purpose. Maybe you've struggled to have kids in the first place. Maybe you've felt that if you can't have children you have no value. Could it be that God is trying to set you free from those mindsets *before* He gives you the desires of your heart? Maybe you're in a completely different stage of life and are dealing with an entirely different set of circumstances.

No matter what you're walking through, that fire is going to serve a purpose. It is meant to refine you. To purify you. To rid you of everything that is holding you back. But keep in mind, that's not the only advantage.

Victory Gains Ground

Did you know that back in biblical times, they had different ways of acquiring land? Today, if we want to buy a piece of property, we can go to the bank, get a loan, and sign some paperwork. Badabing badaboom, the land is yours. And once you've purchased it, it doesn't matter if you literally never touch it again. As long as you have that sheet of paper saying you own it, that's all that matters. Or so we think. But back in biblical times, they did things a little bit differently.

In those days, one of the ways you could acquire a piece of property was by going through a tedious process. First, you would have to set up camp there. Then, you would begin to work the ground. You would till the soil, plant some seeds, and tend to those plants until you saw fruit. At that point, you could go to the government officials and show them proof that you had developed the land and made it better than you found it. They would then reward you by deciding that because you were a good steward of the land, it was best to keep it in your possession.[1]

Here's where I'm going with this. We all hear things about spiritual authority. We go to church and hear sermons about how we can rejoice because we have victory in Jesus. Here's the problem with that: we expect it to be handed to us. Sometimes, having victory over the enemy means you have to go toe to toe with him. Victory is not something we can purchase. Most of us treat it like a modern-day real estate transaction. We think that because we've bought a good piece of property, it should automatically be fruitful, but we're not always willing to put our hands to the plow.

In order for us to see the fruit of our salvation, we have to be willing to steward it. Philippians 2:12-13 says, "Therefore, my

---

1. Bible Hub, "Commentary on Land and Stewardship"

dear friends, as you have always obeyed—not only in my presence, but now much more in my absence—continue to work out your salvation with fear and trembling, for it is God who works in you to will and to act in order to fulfill his good purpose." See? Some things that come with our salvation have to be worked out–with fear and trembling. Yes, victory is a part of it. Authority is a part of it. All of those things have been provided for you as a byproduct of accepting Jesus as your Savior. But just like the Israelites in the wilderness, they had to go out and collect the manna that had been provided for them. Think about it. God is all powerful, right? He can do quite literally anything He wants. So why didn't He just make the manna appear in their mouths? Why didn't He just fill their bellies himself? Why did He make it so that they had to collect it themselves day after day after day? It's because He wanted to partner with them, not control them. And He wants the same for you.

But in order for us to get to the point where you are partnering with God, I need you to understand what this partnership means for you. It means that if you want to have authority over sickness, you're going to have to set up camp in the land of sickness until you see fruit from it. If you want to have dominion in the land of finances, you're going to have to set up camp in the land of lack and work that ground until you see fruit from it. You have authority and dominion over whatever situation you have triumphed over. So whatever situation you are walking through right now is not for your punishment. It is an opportunity for you to take back that land for the kingdom of God.

Shortly after my dad was diagnosed with cancer, I asked my God to teach me more about supernatural healing. I did not realize that praying a prayer like that is like pulling the trigger of a loaded gun. You can't take it back. Over the next five years, my family walked through four different cancer diagnoses, one case of routine surgery gone wrong (leading to four other emergency surgeries), one blood disorder diagnosis, several other surgeries, multiple ER visits, and multiple months of physical therapy, collectively. And that's not even counting all of the health challenges we had with my horse and my other animals. You see, when I prayed that prayer asking Him to teach me about healing, I was just kind of expecting Him to zap me with wisdom. Or, at the very least, point things out to me as I studied scripture. I wasn't expecting to have to get my hands dirty when I didn't even fully understand what was going on.

So many times, we pray for God to help us understand things, but we're expecting to be handed a diploma rather than being handed a textbook and told to study up. We want the finished result, but we don't want to put in the work. After I said that prayer, God plopped me down in the classroom of life where I was about to learn more than I ever bargained for. The funny thing is, He knows I'm a hands-on learner. I didn't learn how to drive a car by being told how to drive a car. I had to get behind the wheel and feel the weight of the pedals for myself. How was I expecting to learn anything without being put in a situation where I would get the chance to practice?

My guess is that whatever He's trying to teach you is going to be learned in a similar way. You're not going to be handed the knowledge on a silver platter. You're not going to be given a fresh crop without participating in the sowing. You're going to be given seeds to plant. You're going to have to roll up your sleeves and get your hands dirty until you see that harvest grow. But the satisfaction you will get from actually experiencing it for yourself will be worth more to you than any knowledge you could find in any book. You're going to see the Bible come to life with your own eyes, and it may be one of the most difficult, but most exciting things you ever experience, as long as you hang in there long enough to reap the reward.

I was recently reflecting on the crazy amount of miracles I was seeing on an almost daily basis. Miracles that I used to fight for and contend for were suddenly falling into my lap. Things that used to take weeks or even months of prayer were suddenly happening after one prayer. My husband would complain about his back hurting, we would say a quick prayer and he would feel better the very next day. I would notice one of my animals walking with a limp and I would pray over them. Before I knew it, they were walking around as if nothing had been bothering them. I was seeing the power of God left and right with what felt like very little effort on my part, and I couldn't seem to figure out why. Then one day, God reminded me, "You've already worked the land, now all you have to do is collect the fruit." Let me assure you, all of your hard work *will* pay off. Set up camp, stay consistent, work the land, collect the fruit.

Don't Let Anyone Steal Your Fruit

While we're on the subject of seeing the fruit of our labor, I've got to share with you one of the visions God gave me to help me understand why we need to contend for things. In this vision, Jesus and I were standing in an orchard full of young fruit trees. Lining the outside of the orchard were rows of people. They couldn't see into the orchard, but I could see them clearly. All of a sudden, they began to pray. As they prayed, the trees began to bloom and produce fruit. The more they prayed, the larger the fruit became. I watched as the fruit grew larger and larger until it was almost ready to pick. Then, out of nowhere, all of these demons flooded into the orchard and started smashing the fruit to the ground. All of the growth that I had just seen take place was obliterated in a matter of a few seconds.

Horrified, I looked to Jesus. "Why would you let them in here?" I asked. "I didn't. My people did," He replied. "Well, can't you kick them out? They're ruining everything!" I cried. "Not if they were invited," he responded. I turned to look at the people. Instead of continuing to pray, they were becoming increasingly frustrated. They started to become bitter and complain. "You said if we prayed, you would answer us! Where's our fruit?!" As their hearts continued to harden, more and more demons flooded the orchard, as if the people's bitterness had just given them an invitation to enter. My heart shattered at the thought that these people were blaming Jesus for what had happened, and even more so that He was letting them.

Sometimes, we get so frustrated in the waiting that we think God isn't moving. We get so irritated with prayers that seem to go unanswered that we just stop asking. But what if those actions are the very thing that are contributing to our downfall? What if we chose to keep contending for things, even when all hope looks lost?

Now, I want to set the record straight. I am encouraging you to contend for things in prayer. I am imploring you to go to war against the schemes of the enemy. But I am in no way suggesting that you get to determine what fruit grows on that tree. You see, just because we contend for things doesn't mean we are trying to determine the outcome. The dictionary definition for contending means "to struggle to surmount."[2] In other words, to struggle *in order to* overcome. But as we've already discussed, victory doesn't always mean that our circumstances change in our favor.

I remember the first time I really contended for something in prayer. Earlier, I mentioned my dad's cancer diagnosis that he received in 2020. At that point, I didn't know God that well. I didn't know if He would heal my dad or not. And I knew that there was no magic button I could press to make God give me a miracle. All I could do was pray. For hours a day, I prayed for my dad. But let me be clear. I wasn't praying to try and *make* God

---

2. Oxford Languages, s.v. "contend," in Oxford English Dictionary.

heal him. I was praying so that if my dad's life ended, I would be at peace. If my dad had been taken from us, I would have known that I had done everything in my power to stop it. The second half of James 4:2 says, "You do not have because you do not ask God." If my dad didn't receive his healing, it wasn't going to be because I didn't ask. So I asked. And I asked again. For months on end.

It seems like King David had a similar approach when he was contending for the life of his son. In 2 Samuel 12, we're told the story of Bathsheba giving birth to David's son. Shortly after, the child gets sick. I want you to see how David responds to this unfortunate situation. Look at what happens in verses 16-22:

> David pleaded with God for the child. He fasted and spent the nights lying in sackcloth on the ground. The elders of his household stood beside him to get him up from the ground, but he refused, and he would not eat any food with them. On the seventh day the child died. David's attendants were afraid to tell him that the child was dead, for they thought, "While the child was still living, he wouldn't listen to us when we spoke to him. How can we now tell him the child is dead? He may do something desperate." David noticed that his attendants were whispering among themselves, and he realized the child was dead. "Is the child dead?" he asked. "Yes," they replied, "he is dead." Then David got up from the ground. After he had

> washed, put on lotions and changed his clothes, he went into the house of the Lord and worshiped. Then he went to his own house, and at his request they served him food, and he ate. His attendants asked him, "Why are you acting this way? While the child was alive, you fasted and wept, but now that the child is dead, you get up and eat!" He answered, "While the child was still alive, I fasted and wept. I thought, 'Who knows? The Lord may be gracious to me and let the child live.' But now that he is dead, why should I go on fasting? Can I bring him back again? I will go to him, but he will not return to me."

It seems as though David was approaching the situation the same way I was. He knew that he couldn't control whether the child lived or died, but his knowledge of the Father's love for him made him brave enough to ask. Once the child was dead, he was at peace, because he knew he had done everything he could to prevent it.

Now, I want you to stick with me because I know this seems confusing. You may be wondering why we should even contend for things if we can't determine the outcome. What's the point in praying if God has already decided what He's going to do and nothing we do or say can influence it? Where was David's victory? Remember what I said at the very beginning of this book? About how sometimes God hides His victories behind a veil of defeat?

That's exactly what seems to be happening here, so let's pull back that curtain.

Whenever people confide in me about issues they are having in their marriage, I always like to remind them of this one thing: The fight is not you versus your spouse, the fight is you and your spouse versus the problem. Sometimes we forget that we are meant to fight as a team. That we are meant to work together to solve the issues that are causing distance to come between us. As the bride of Christ, it's no different. When we contend for things in prayer, we are not engaging in a battle of wills. We are not stomping our feet like a defiant toddler, demanding our way until our Father caves to our demands. We are fighting the problem.

Now that you have that perspective, let's take a look at this story from a different angle. What was the main issue in David's life at this point in time? It was distance from God. The whole reason Bathsheba conceived this child in the first place was because David was not doing what he was supposed to be doing. He was supposed to be off at war, fighting with his people, not at home sleeping with married women. Even if David still loved and served God, a part of him had grown distant from the Father's heart. When David contended for his son's life, those prayers were solving the issue at hand: David's distance from God. That situation drove him back into his Father's arms.

When my dad received his diagnosis, the biggest issue in my life was that I had only known God through the distorted lens of religion, and not through a personal relationship. So when I contended in prayer for my dad, what were those prayers really doing? They were solving the issue at hand. It was bringing me into a relationship with the Father, without the obligation of organized religion. Do you see what I'm saying? David and I both contended for the same thing. We both contended for the life of a loved one. And yet, we received very different outcomes. But did we both receive a victory? Yes! Because we both were driven into a deeper relationship with God Himself. Sometimes contending for things in prayer is not so that we can achieve a desired outcome, but so that those prayers can change us from the inside out. We don't always get what we want as a result of prayer, but we always seem to be given what we need the most.

Now, I'm not saying that God caused my dad's cancer as a twisted way of forcing me to come closer to Him. God is not some sinister puppeteer, pulling at the strings of our lives so that He can get what He wants. All I'm saying is that sometimes God will *use* what the enemy tries to throw our way as the means to justify a more desirable end result.

There is an ancient Japanese art for restoring broken pottery called Kintsugi. This method involves fixing cracks in the pottery or welding broken pieces back together by using a gold colored resin. Rather than hiding the cracks or imperfections, this method highlights the beauty of restoring something that once seemed beyond repair, and making it even more valuable than it was before. Sometimes, it seems like that's what God is doing in our own lives. The devil is going around attempting to smash our lives to pieces, making us believe that we are no longer useful, that we are broken beyond repair. Meanwhile, God is coming right behind him, putting those pieces back together with an even stronger bond. God may not have caused the breakage, but sometimes He will use the breakage to teach us that there is quite literally nothing He cannot fix.

Victory Isn't Just for You

Did you know that one single apple seed can produce up to 12,000 apples? That one seed turns into one apple tree. That one apple tree goes through season after season, producing more fruit each year than it ever has before. That one tree will produce approximately 12,000 apples over the course of its lifetime.[3] Isn't that wild? You'd never think that such a seemingly insignificant seed could produce such a drastic impact.

You already know where I'm going with this don't you? You are that seed. Yes, for a time, you'll feel like you're buried. But that season will lead to new growth, which will lead to fruit, which will lead to people being fed by your testimony, which will lead to more seeds being planted. Think about how many people you encounter on a daily basis. What if just one of those people every day was impacted by your life, whether you knew it or not? How much fruit do you think that would produce as a result of you not giving up on yourself? Here's the truth. You matter. Your life matters. Your story matters. There's someone who needs to hear

---

3. TreeFluent, *How Many Apples Grow on Trees?*, 2024.

your testimony because it's going to help them get through their darkest valley.

Here's the thing I want you to understand. Your path doesn't just affect you. Every time we walk through something difficult, we have the opportunity to bring others out with us just by sharing how we made it through. The first half of Revelation 12:11 says, "They triumphed over him by the blood of the Lamb and by the word of their testimony." That means that every single time we share our testimony with someone who needs it, we are declaring victory over the devil. However, on the flip side, if we always take the easy route, always look for another way out, we will be spared of the difficulties, yes, but others may be spared of their rescue.

Just think about what happened with Lot and Abraham. Abraham has a moment where he realizes that the land they are currently occupying cannot support both his herd and his nephew Lot's herd without fights breaking out among the shepherds. So, they decided to part ways. This is what happened in Genesis 13:8-11.

> So Abram said to Lot, "Let's not have any quarreling between you and me, or between your herders and mine, for we are close relatives. Is not the whole land before you? Let's part company. If you go to the left, I'll go to the right; if you go to the right, I'll go to the left." Lot looked around and saw that the whole plain of the Jordan toward Zoar was well watered, like the garden of the Lord, like the land of

> Egypt. (This was before the Lord destroyed Sodom and Gomorrah.) So Lot chose for himself the whole plain of the Jordan and set out toward the east. The two men parted company.

I can just picture it now. Lot and Abraham are standing on a dusty road that stretches out for miles in front of them, completely dividing the land in half. On the left side of the road, the grass is almost completely brown. That grass looks like it hasn't seen water in a month. On the right side of the road, however, it looks like the people who live there have been turning on the sprinklers daily. That grass is so healthy, it looks like plush green carpet that you can curl up and take a nap on. Lot doesn't even seem to hesitate in his choice. He takes the easy path. The path of least resistance. It seems good to him at the time. This path seems to guarantee that his livestock will be well-fed, which means that he can make a lot of money from them, which means that his family will be well-fed. What could possibly go wrong?

What we don't see is that when we choose the path of least resistance, we compromise. We neglect to realize that the struggle is what produces perseverance. I'm sure that when Lot chose that green pasture, he didn't know that he was choosing the path that would ultimately lead to his wife's death. I'm sure he didn't think that this path would eventually traumatize his daughters and make their future incredibly difficult. But that's the issue. He wasn't thinking about the future. He was thinking about what would be easiest right now, not knowing the consequences that would bring later down the road.

On the other hand, there's another story in the Bible that shows us what happens when we choose the path that is not always easy. In Daniel 6, we see that Daniel has been appointed to serve under the king. The problem was that the other administrators didn't seem to like Daniel very much. So, they devised a plan to get him killed. They tricked the king into making a law stating that no one was allowed to pray to anyone except the king. They knew good and well that Daniel prayed to God three times a day, like clockwork. Daniel soon became aware of this law. At this point, he had a choice to make. He could either take the easy path and hide his prayer life, maybe choosing to only pray in his head, rather than praying out loud. Or, he could continue to love God, out loud, as he always had, knowing that it could get him killed. Regardless, he chose the latter.

Once the other administrators found out about this, they told the king, who was forced to sentence Daniel to the lion's den. We all know what happens next, right? God shut the mouth of the lions and Daniel's life was spared. Hooray! Sometimes I think we forget the magnitude of this story because we've heard it so many times. But I really want you to think about it. When Daniel prays out loud, he knows that he is risking death. But not just any death. He is risking being torn limb from limb by vicious wild animals. He is risking a painful, traumatic death. And yet, he chooses to pray anyway. Now, watch what happens next in verses 25 and 26. "Then King Darius wrote to all the nations and peoples of every language in all the earth: 'May you prosper greatly! I issue a decree that in every part of my kingdom people must fear and reverence the God of Daniel. For he is the living God and he endures forever; his kingdom will not be destroyed, his dominion will never end."

By refusing to take the easy path, Daniel was risking his own life, yes, but he was also clearing the way for an entire kingdom to be turned back to God. If Daniel had taken the easy path, his whole nation would've been forcefully led away from their Father's arms. Daniel was willing to lay down his life for a cause that he believed in. We have to ask ourselves, are we willing to do the same?

God once gave me a vision that illustrates this point, too. I know, I know. I get a lot of visions. It's just the way that He helps my creative brain make sense of things. In this vision, there was a line of about five or six people, myself included. We were all standing in front of a river of mud with a cute little wooden bridge over the top of it. On the other side of the mud puddle was God. One by one, He would call the people to come to him, and one at a time, they would cross over the wooden bridge and stand at His side. Finally, it was my turn. But when He called me, He took me by surprise. He said, "Okay, Caitlin. Now, I want you to come to Me. But I don't want you to use the bridge. I want you to go through the mud." *What?! That's not fair!* I thought to myself. I had just watched all of these people cross over this bridge, perfectly happy and dry on the other side. And yet, I wasn't allowed to follow that same path. Regardless, I obeyed, because let's be honest, if God told me to jump on one foot, pat my head, and rub my belly at the same time, I would do it.

So off into the mud I went. It took me a lot longer to get across the river. The mud was thick and as I reached the middle, it came all the way up to my ribcage. One small step at a time, I made my way across. As I waded halfway through the river, I saw these hands begin to emerge from the mud and grab onto me, but they weren't trying to pull me under. More and more hands came out of the dirty water and clung to my clothes. Carrying their weight made my movements even slower and more difficult. But, finally, I heard their gasping breath as I realized what was happening. I wasn't just going through the mud, I was rescuing people out of it.

Once I finally made it to the other side, I had as many people with me as I could possibly carry. Exhausted but relieved, I looked up at God. He gave me a knowing smile as if to say *Now, do you see?* The whole point of our refinement isn't just to get through it. We're not just given these trials so that we can become better people. We are on one giant rescue mission. Our whole goal is to bring as many people as we can with us. And if that means we have to go through more difficult things for that to happen, so be it. Because this life is not about our comfort. There will be plenty of time for that when we get to heaven. In order for us to be effective here, we have to keep that mission at the forefront of our mind.

John 15:13 says, "Greater love has no one than this: to lay down one's life for one's friends." To me, that doesn't always mean physically ending our lives for the sake of those around us. Sometimes, it looks like intentionally sacrificing our comfortable lives, our easy lives, our worry-free lives for the benefit of the people we love. Sometimes choosing to take the more difficult path results in a greater harvest than we could ever imagine, we just have to be willing to brave it.

In order to do that, you need to realize that you are not insignificant. What you do with this life matters. And it's about time you know that you don't have to live in defeat anymore. It's time to rise up, shake off those old mindsets, and face your challenges head on, because you never know whose life could be impacted by your decision to do just that.

Anointed to Win

I once heard a sermon that revolved around the passage of Deuteronomy 28.[4] This passage talks about all of the blessings that are attached to our obedience to God. If you have kids, you understand this principle. You don't make your kids earn your love with their obedience. Your love is a free gift that you give them simply because of who they are and how much they mean to you. However, we do have a natural tendency to reward our kids a little extra for their good behavior.

Imagine you have two children. One is incredibly obedient, and the other is not. Maybe you have one child who is quick to listen and does as they're told because they understand that part of your role is to protect them and that it is in their best

4. Sermon by Pastor Troy Brewer, OpenDoor Church, Burleson, Texas.

interest to listen to you. On the other hand, you may have another child who thinks they know what is best and, as a result of that, they constantly buck against everything you say. Would you love those two children any differently? Of course not. You would show love to both of those children regardless of their behavior. However, you would probably reward their behavior differently even though you love them the same.

The same is true with God. He is our loving Father after all. That love extends to all of his children without discrimination. However, as outlined in Deuteronomy 28, there are certain rewards attached to our obedience. As I was listening to this sermon, something really interesting stuck out to me. The preacher described these blessings as an "anointing to win."

So many times, when we think about God's blessings, we tend to think of the stuff. My health is intact, so I must be blessed by God. I live in a nice house and all my bills are paid. It must be the blessings and favor of God on my life. We think that if we are obedient to God's plan for our life, he will reward us with health, wealth, and an easy path. While he is a good Father who absolutely can give us those good things, more often than not, the blessing is not about the stuff. It's the anointing to win. The blessing of God is not an object, it's an ability. An ability to be prosperous in any situation you're placed in because you know who has your back.

When we look at the blessings of God as the stuff we have or don't have, it's easy to get discouraged, to feel unfulfilled, and to slip back into that place of defeat. But when we look at it as an anointing to make it through any hardship we face and come out stronger on the other side, that's when we start living from a place of victory. That's when we start to understand when the first half of Isaiah 54:17 says, "no weapon forged against you will prevail." It doesn't mean that the weapons won't be forged. It doesn't mean that we will have a cushy life where we never have to fight another battle. It means that with each and every battle we face, we can rest assured that we will come out of the other side victorious. Because there's one thing you need to remember about leaving defeat and stepping into a place of victory; the most victorious people are not the ones who never lose, but the ones who never quit.

Epilogue

So, what comes next? You've worked through all of these broken mindsets and you've been equipped to keep fighting. Now what do you do? Surely, you don't think the journey ends there, do you? Absolutely not. This is where the fun actually begins. This is where you step into your purpose and run the race set before you with absolutely nothing to hold you back. This is where you experience the true freedom that Christ died to give you. Now, this doesn't mean that things will be easy from here on out. Running is exhausting no matter how conditioned you are, but it's a whole lot easier without heavy chains strapped to your ankles. Now, you'll get to experience what it looks like to go farther and faster than you've ever imagined, and gain ground for the kingdom along the way.

It's Okay to Mess Up

Of all of the disciples in the Bible, my favorite has to be Peter. He's just so relatable. Here he is, trying his best to please Jesus, and tripping over his own feet as he does it. Of course, Jesus' example is the one that we should always try to emulate, but I'm thankful that we are also given Peter's example to give us an idea of what it looks like to fail miserably and still be loved deeply. Try as we might to do the right thing, we are flawed human beings who are inevitably going to mess up.

Do you want to know what I love the most about Peter? He never gives up. He never seems to get complacent, or get stuck in the same cycles over and over again. He acknowledges when he's wrong, learns from his mistakes, and keeps moving forward. Peter gives me hope. He makes me believe that truly anyone can be transformed by the love of God as long as they are willing to partner with Him. Peter paints the picture of God's grace and patience, and how He's willing to stick with us even when we fumble time and time again.

I'm sure you've had times in your life where you've felt like you've made too big of a mess to be cleaned up. You may feel like your life is in shambles, that your own mind is fighting against your freedom, that you keep messing up no matter how many times you try. And then you look at Peter and see that he messed up too. He tried to talk Jesus out of going to the cross. He nearly drowned after he experienced what it was like to walk on the waves. He denied Jesus after all the time they had spent together. And maybe that gives you the courage to keep going. Because maybe, like me, Peter helps you realize that we serve a gracious God who doesn't want you to give up. Even with all of the mistakes that Peter made, Jesus still said to him, "And I tell you that you are Peter, and on this rock I will build my church, and the gates of Hades will not overcome it." (Matthew 16:18). Like a parent waiting for their child to learn to walk, He doesn't care how many times you stumble. He doesn't care if you cry or need to be held when it feels too difficult to get back up again. He just wants you to keep trying. And He's celebrating every little victory with you along the way.

Daring to Change

One thing we see through Peter's story is that his transformation took years to develop. We're first introduced to him when he is fishing. Jesus performs a miracle by telling him to cast his nets on the other side of the boat. Peter and his men haul in more fish than their boats can carry, despite not having caught anything all night. Jesus then invites him to become a fisher of men. This is where Peter's journey begins. Like a caterpillar hatching out of its egg, Peter emerges into a new life, ready to eat and grow. For the next three years, he is fed by Jesus' teaching and examples. And as he applies these principles to his life, we see his character begin to mature little by little.

However, Peter's transformation didn't happen until after Jesus' resurrection and ascension. Once the Holy Spirit arrives at Pentecost, that's when Peter's true metamorphosis begins. All of a sudden, he seems like an entirely different person. Rather than asking questions and debating with people, he is answering questions and restoring peace. He begins to preach and see thousands of people come to accept Christ. He sees miracle after miracle take place. He steps into his true identity.

As amazing as his story is to read, it never would have been possible if Peter hadn't dared to be different. He had to become different from the past versions of himself, and different from the world around him. If Peter had remained in the same cycles that he was used to, he never would've been able to play the same part in the story of the gospel being spread worldwide. In all actuality, we may never have even read about him if he had chosen to stay stuck. But he didn't. As scary and unfamiliar as it was, he took that step. And then he took another. And another. Every time he was corrected, he took it to heart. Every time he was given an opportunity, he pounced on it. And just look at the outcome.

What do you think would happen if you do the same? What do you think your life would look like if you let go of the person you've always known and became the person you were always intended to be? My guess is that we might be reading a story about you one day. About how God used your willingness and your bravery to write another incredible story. Let me tell you something, friend. God isn't looking for perfect people, He's just looking for willing people. People who say yes to breaking free from the same old patterns. People who are willing to get out of the boat and step onto the waves, knowing good and well they could sink. People like Peter, who don't let their mistakes and struggles define them, but who let their Creator define them. I'm willing to bet that you're one of them. Clearly, you don't shy away from hard topics. You don't throw in the towel when things get tough. Like Peter, you are willing to keep going, no matter the cost. And like Peter, God will use you in a mighty way because of it.

Daring to be Different from the World

My husband's grandfather (by choice, not by blood) always says, "You've got to be different to make a difference."[1] Nobody changes the status quo by going with the flow and blending in with the masses. If you want to make an impact in the world around you, you're going to have to be willing to separate yourself from it. Peter seemed to understand this. After he received the Holy Spirit at Pentecost, he no longer blended in. He no longer wanted to. He received a taste of the freedom and power that came from that radical transformation and there was no going back. He was willing to get arrested and even die for what he believed. But that was what separated him from the world around him. He no longer chose to conform.

I can remember the first time I truly heard God speaking to me. I was around 15 or 16 years old. I was an angsty teenager, struggling to fit in. It seemed as though everyone around me had a mold that they wanted me to conform to and I didn't fit inside a single one of them. As I was anxiously pacing around my yard, I thought to myself, *Why can't I just be normal?* All of a sudden, an image popped into my mind. It was a picture of a single yellow

1. Quote by Kent Yarbrough.

wildflower in a field of red roses. Then I heard the words, "You are different. I made you that way on purpose. And one day, you're going to see what that purpose is."

There I was, trying so desperately to fit into the boxes that everyone else thought I should belong to, when all along, God had set me apart for something greater. My guess is that you probably felt a lot like I did. Everyone who has ever felt defeated has arrived there because they felt like they couldn't get anything right. You've probably faced a lot of opposition by being told who you should be, what you should do, or how you should behave. And you felt like you didn't measure up.

What if I told you that you're not just different, but set apart for a crucial role in a larger story? But in order to step into that purpose, you're going to have to be willing to look like an idiot at times. Moses had to risk looking like an idiot as he raised his staff towards the Red Sea. Joshua and the Israelites had to risk looking like idiots as they marched around Jericho day after day while the people inside those walls laughed at them. But when it comes to the things of God, there's nothing truly beneficial about playing it safe.

When it comes to the insect world, most bugs spend a large amount of time building homes for themselves. Wasps create nests, bees slave over the safety of their hives, and ants dedicate nearly their entire lives to creating intricate underground tunnels to survive in. Do you know which insect doesn't build a home? Butterflies. They're different. The rest of the bugs probably laugh at them and call them morons for not creating a place for themselves to get out of the rain or shelter from predators. But do you want to know why they don't build homes? It's because they spend the entirety of their time on a mission. They don't have time to get comfortable. They are here for a limited amount of time and they aren't going to waste it by hunkering down and creating the illusion of safety.

Matthew 6:19-21 says, "Do not store up for yourselves treasures on earth, where moths and vermin destroy, and where thieves break in and steal. But store up for yourselves treasures in heaven, where moths and vermin do not destroy, and where thieves do not break in and steal. For where your treasure is, there your heart will be also." It's tempting for us to want to seek a life of ease and comfort and predictability. We all want to create cozy little nests for ourselves where we can shut out the rest of the world and the pain that comes with it. To protect ourselves from those who want to hurt us or the storms that may come our way. But when we focus all of our efforts on creating predictable, comfortable, safe spaces for ourselves, we rob ourselves of a greater purpose.

Stay on Mission

When its transformation is complete, the butterfly steps into a far greater purpose in the ecosystem than it once could. You see, butterflies are pollinators. Meaning that they help spread the pollen that the plants around them need in order to grow. If the butterfly were to waste its valuable, fleeting time making themselves comfortable, they would miss out on the very purpose they were created for in the first place.

Like the butterfly, you were created for a greater purpose than you can even imagine. You may not be able to see what lies ahead of you, but God does. He designed you with a specific plan for your life. All He's asking is that you will say yes to it. That you will continue to walk towards it. And that you will allow Him to lead you into a life that you never thought was possible.

In Matthew 28:19-20 ISV (emphasis added), Jesus says this: "Therefore, *as you go*, disciple people in all nations, baptizing them in the name of the Father, and the Son, and the Holy Spirit, teaching them to obey everything that I've commanded you. And remember, I am with you each and every day until the end of the age." Sometimes I think that we get confused about what staying on mission really means. I used to think it meant that I needed to preach on street corners and pray for strangers everywhere I went. And while there is nothing at all wrong with that, daily discipleship looks a little different.

Remember when I said that butterflies are pollinators? They flit around from flower to flower, plant to plant. And *as they go*, they are spreading the very thing that those plants need for survival. Our job is not to transform people. That's the Holy Spirit's job. Our job is simply to give people the information and examples that they need to point them back to the one who transformed us in the first place. 1 Corinthians 3:7 says, "So neither the one who plants nor the one who waters is anything, but only God, who makes things grow." Don't put too much pressure on yourself if you don't see the change in those around you right away. Growth takes time. Just remember that everyday is an opportunity. Every person that you encounter gives you a chance to plant a seed. Every smile or kind word or selfless act of good will serves as a road map to point others back to Jesus.

Living out your victory simply means that you are free to help others discover theirs. You are no longer bound. No longer trapped. No longer stuck. You've left defeat in the rearview mirror. Welcome to the land of victory. This isn't your finish line, this is your starting point. And I, for one, can't wait to see what you do next.

Acknowledgements

To my husband,

Thank you for always being understanding and supportive. Thank you for allowing me the time to write when the creativity is flowing, and for talking me through writer's block. Thank you for being steady and for helping me through every storm I face. Thank you for always believing in me, even when I don't believe in myself. Thank you for loving me well. I meant what I said in the beginning. It truly is an honor to be your wife.

To my kids,

Being your mom is one of the greatest things I've ever done with my life. No matter how many books I write, you will always be my favorite creations. I can't wait to watch you grow into the people God has called you to be. I know He has amazing plans for you. Thank you for always having a hug ready for me, and I promise to always have one ready for you.

To my family,

Thank you to my mom and mother-in-law for always being willing to fix my atrocious grammar mistakes and help me shape these stories. My books would not be what they are without you. Thank you to my dad, who has always been in awe of my creativity and keeps my books permanently on his nightstand. Thank you to my father-in-law, who is always ready and willing to dissect spiritual topics with me. Thank you to my siblings (both by blood and by marriage) who are in constant support of my journey. And to my grandmother who always wants updates on my projects so she can tell me what a great job I'm doing. Your encouragement does more for me than you will ever know.

To Robert and Amanda Andrews,

Thank you for being a constant source of encouragement and comfort throughout this entire process, and for your feedback that made this book ten times more powerful. But even more than that, thank you for your friendship. To say that you've radically changed my life would be an understatement. I thank God for your entire family daily.

To Alvin Foster,

Thank you for never putting limitations on my creativity, and for always helping me bring my ideas to life. From book cover designs to tech help to pep talks (so many pep talks), I know I can always count on you. Your friendship is invaluable to me.

To Shayla Huber,

I'm so thankful for your constant willingness to read every single word I write and to challenge me when I need it. You continually push me to new heights (even when it makes me uncomfortable!) and encourage me never to settle for less than God's best for my life.

To my Elevate Church Family,

Thank you for always treating me like I belong. Thank you for loving me well, even in (especially in) the messy moments. You've truly shown me what it looks like for a church to be the body of Christ. I'm so grateful to be a part of your family.

To my readers,

We've been on quite a journey together, haven't we? When God first asked me to start sharing what I was learning on TikTok, I had no idea that a few years later, it would lead to this. None of it would be possible without your continued support. Thank you for allowing me to share what I'm learning as I go, no matter how messy the journey may be. I hope that we can stay on this course together for many years to come.

About the Author

Caitlin Childs is a wife, mother, author and speaker. She is a gifted storyteller who makes even the most difficult concepts easy to understand through the use of analogies and examples. She is passionate about helping people grow one step closer to God by sharing her own personal discoveries and lessons learned along her faith journey.

Follow her journey on TikTok, Instagram, and YouTube, or by visiting yourfriendcaitlin.com

Also by

In her first book, *7 Days to a Life of Limitless,* Caitlin shared her perspective on moving from a place of religious obligation to a place of personal relationship with Jesus. Her personal stories and analogies resonated deeply with readers, gaining this title over 500 positive reviews within the first year of it's publication. All of Caitlin's books can be purchased on Amazon, TikTok shop, or at yourfriendcaitlin.com.

Made in the USA
Coppell, TX
28 March 2026

74286867R00144